DECORATE LIFE :

CELEBRATIONS

CONTENTS

Celebrate all year long with this must-have inspirational resource.
Now, start Decorating Life.

DECORATE LIFE : CELEBRATIONS

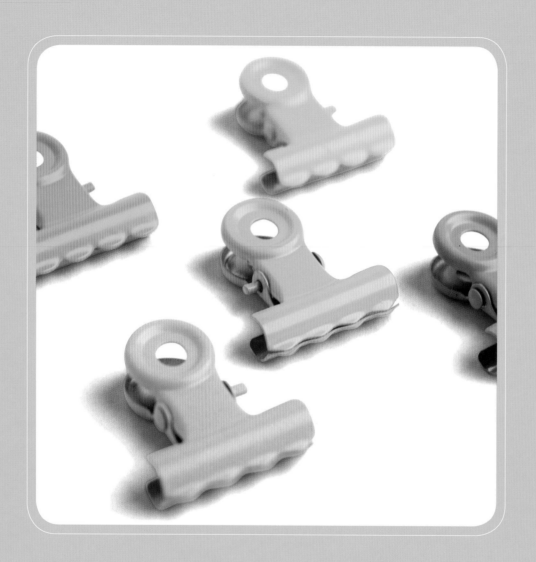

1
BIRTHDAYS

GIRLFRIENDS' LUNCHEON

STICK TO A SINGLE COLOR THEME FOR A POLISHED LOOK

GIRLFRIENDS LUNCH INVITE BY MARGIE ROMNEY-ASLETT

(TIP)

USE DECORATIVE SCISSORS TO FINISH EDGE

(TIP)

BEAUTIFY BATH PRODUCTS FOR
SPECIALIZED PARTY FAVORS

RELAX I. TO RELEASE
TENSION 2. *to* ~~r~~
from work 3. to ~~b~~
at ease 4. *to rele*~~a~~
physical or men~~ta~~
pressures from o~~n~~

Friendship
the state of being

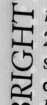

BRIGHT 1. *shining with light*
2. brilliant in color or
sound; vivid **3. lively &**
cheerful 4. *favorable;*
hopeful 5. illustrious

CAPTURED MOMENTS

COMBINE ONE STRONG PHOTO AND HEARTFELT JOURNALING

I COULD NOT LOVE YOU MORE BY MELLETTE BEREZOSKI

So you are five today.

And you know that on every birthday, Mama gets a little emotional. You are such a big boy now, going to school and learning so much, playing soccer and basketball, helping Daddy with the vegetable garden, and doing your chores. I am so very proud of you, son. You are the sweetest little boy I have ever known, and I knew you would be even before you were born. You reassured me last night that you would still be my baby. "Even when I'm a grown up", you promised me. My cute little boy, you are always so sweet to me. I often ask myself how I ever managed without you; the concept of life before you seems so foreign. But there is one thing I am absolutely sure of: today and every day, I could not love you any more than I already do. **Happy 5th Birthday, son.**

Dayton 03/15/06

i could not love you more

(TIP)
ADHERE LARGE NUMBER USING FOAM TAPE

Come join the fun!

five

Dayton's 5th Birthday Party

Sunday, March 5, 2006
1:00 pm - 3:00 pm
Crosby Community Park
RSVP: 832.123.4567

thanks

thank YOU

grazie

(TIP)
FILL ROLLS WITH CANDY, CRAYONS, STICKERS AND SMALL TOYS

DAY TO REMEMBER

LET A COORDINATING COLOR PALETTE CARRY OUT THE THEME

PICTURE YOURSELF AT MY PARTY BY ERIN TERRELL

Picture Yourself at
Daisy's 9th Birthday Party.

your
photo
here

Saturday, November 25th
4:00 PM
at Libby Lu

Come ready for a full
Fashion Makeover and Photo Shoot!!
(bring this camera so you can take photos
home for your scrapbook)

PARTY
TIME

(TIP)
ADD MINI FRAME TO INVITATION AND TIE WITH RIBBON

(TIP)
DRESS UP A DISPOSABLE CAMERA OR CAMERA BOX
TO COORDINATE WITH INVITATIONS

PLAYFUL FAVORS
ADD INSTANT SPARKLE TO YOUR EMBELLISHMENTS WITH PAINT AND GLITTER

OUR SHINING STAR GIFT BOX AND BUCKET BY ROBYN WERLICH

(TIP)
FOR PARTY FAVORS, GLUE STRIP
OF CARDSTOCK TO PIXIE STICK
WITH GUESTS' NAMES

COMBINE PAPER AND TRIM FOR A PLAYFUL BIRTHDAY CARD

OUR SHINING STAR CARD BY ROBYN WERLICH

Our **Shining Star** is turning 3!!!
Come celebrate the birthday of

Hudson Werlich

with us on
April 23, 2007
5-8 p.m.
Pizza and Cake will be served
@ the Werlich home

(TIP)
EXPERIMENTING WITH COMPUTER TYPE
CAN ADD PERSONALITY TO A SIMPLE CARD

SUSPENDED INVITATION

MAKE A FRAME WITHIN A FRAME USING PHOTO TAGS AND TWINE

PARTY INVITE BY JENNIFER JENSEN

(TIP)
UTILIZE AS A PARTY INVITATION OR PLACE CARD

PHOTO PLACEMAT
PAPER-FRAMED PICTURES DOUBLE AS PLACEMATS

PARTY PLACEMAT BY JENNIFER JENSEN

(TIP)

ADD A DECORATIVE FOAM STAMP TO BACK OF GLASS PLATES

SURPRISE, SURPRISE

HIDDEN PULLOUT REVEALS ALL THE SECRET PARTY DETAILS

SHH . . . BY MAGGIE HOLMES

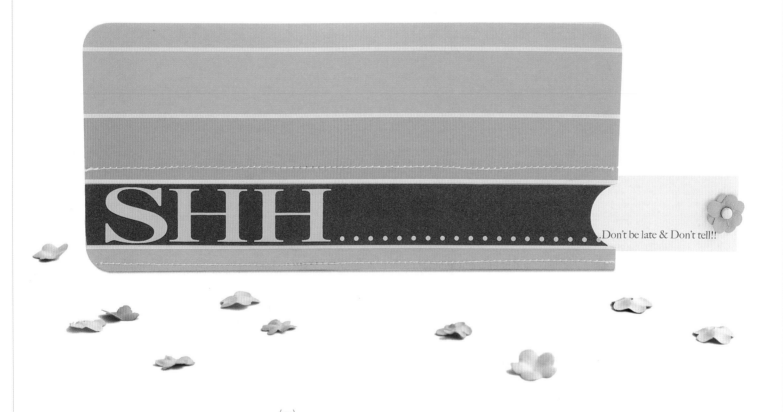

SHH.........................Don't be late & Don't tell!!

(TIP)
STITCH POCKET USING SEWING MACHINE

menu

drink
cherry lemonade

salad
mixed greens with shallot vinaigrette

kellie

mash...   ...ons
citrus marinated pork chops

dessert
old fashioned apple pie
caramel ice cream

. . . .

(TIP)
ADD EXTRA FLAIR TO TABLE BY UTILIZING
DIFFERENT RIBBON COLORS AND STYLES

COVERED MONOGRAM

WRAP LETTER WITH PAPER, CREATING A LARGE CARD ATTENDEES CAN SIGN

CELEBRATE MONOGRAM LETTER BY ROBYN WERLICH

(TIP)
ADD VERBIAGE, BRADS AND EMBELLISHMENTS

YEARS YOUNG

LAYER PAPER PATTERNS FOR FESTIVE BIRTHDAY EMBELLISHMENTS

CELEBRATE CARD AND FAVOR BOXES BY ROBYN WERLICH

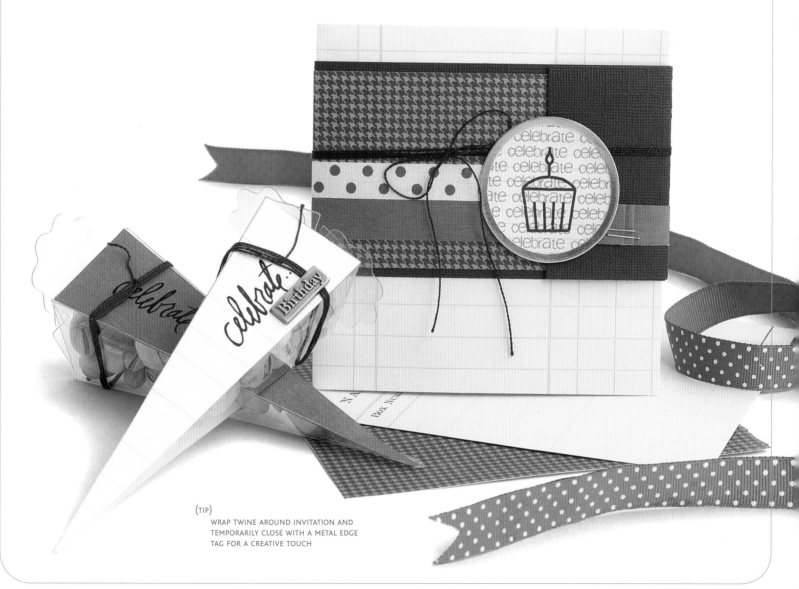

(TIP)

WRAP TWINE AROUND INVITATION AND
TEMPORARILY CLOSE WITH A METAL EDGE
TAG FOR A CREATIVE TOUCH

2
WEDDING

SHOWERED IN STYLE
BOHO CHIC ADDS MODERN ELEGANCE TO INVITATIONS

BRIDAL SHOWER INVITATION BY MELLETTE BEREZOSKI

Please join us for a
bridal shower
honoring

ie Marshall

urday, May 27, 2006
'clock in the afternoon
ome of Mellette Berezoski
1234 Maple Drive

dly reply by May 24th
832.123.4567

e bride is registered at
Pottery Barn
Crate & Barrel

(TIP)
ROUND TOP CORNERS OF FRONT FLAPS
ALLOWING HINT OF INSIDE TO SHOW

EXCEPTIONALLY GIFTED

UNIQUE FAVORS MAKE LASTING IMPRESSIONS

JULIE AND ALAN BY MELLETTE BEREZOSKI

(TIP)
USE HINGES TO CONNECT FRAME TO PHOTO

Julie and Alan &

To *love* someone is to see a *miracle* invisible to others.
"Francois Mauriac"

TULLE WRAPS

SEW AND FILL TULLE TUBES WITH CANDY AND A RUB-ON SENTIMENT

WEDDING FAVOR BY LONI STEVENS

(TIP)
WOVEN RIBBON COMPLIMENTS TULLE
WITHOUT OVERWHELMING THE DESIGN

VISUAL DIMENSION

EMBOSSING CREATES AN ELEGANT ELEMENT AS WELL AS DEPTH

WEDDING INVITATION BY LONI STEVENS

(TIP)

SIMPLE INVITATION BECOMES EXTRAORDINARY WITH
ADDITION OF MINI BLOSSOMS, GEMS AND BRADS

BUDDING ROMANCE

PAINT TURNS INEXPENSIVE GLASS VASES
INTO STUNNING CENTERPIECES

PAINTED BUD VASE BY JULIE TURNER

(TIP)

DRYING TIMES CAN BE LONG FOR TALL,
NARROW BUD VASES, SO PLAN AHEAD

SIGN IN

LEAVE WELL-WISHES IN SMALL GUEST BOOKS
PLACED AT EACH TABLE

WEDDING GUEST BOOKS BY JULIE TURNER

(TIP)
AFTER THE WEDDING, SLIP A PHOTO OF
GUESTS INSIDE THEIR TABLE'S MINI BOOK

GUEST BOOK

table
3

NEW BEGINNING
PRESERVE THE MAGIC OF THE MOMENT
WEDDING MEMOIR BY KEISHA CAMPBELL

(TIP)
ENHANCE PHOTOS WITH UNIQUE
PAPER PATTERNS AND COLORS

(TIP) SOFT EYE-CATCHING COLORS AND PATTERNS
ARE JUST RIGHT FOR SPECIAL UNIONS

NUPTIAL NOTIONS
COORDINATED ELEMENTS TIE THEME TOGETHER

LOVE CANDLE HOLDERS AND GUESTS' TABLE NUMBERS BY JENNIFER JENSEN

(TIP)

PLACE ITEMS THAT MATCH WEDDING
THEME AROUND CANDLE BASE AND
TABLE NUMBER

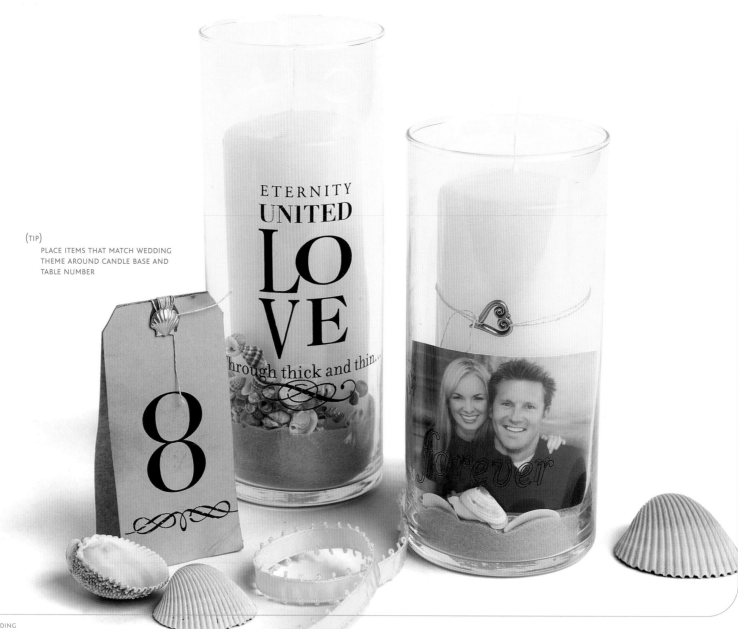

SCROLLED ANNOUNCEMENT
USE PAPER AND BAMBOO STICKS FOR A NON-TRADITIONAL INVITATION AND FAN
WEDDING INVITATION AND MONOGRAM FAN BY JENNIFER JENSEN

M

a perfect shell is a gift from the sea

as beautiful and unique

as our love is meant to be

PLEASE JOIN US AS WE
SARAH STANGER
&
TEREL MATTHEWS
JOIN OUR LIVES IN MARRIAGE
SATURDAY THE EIGHTH OF JULY, 2006
AT FIVE O'CLOCK IN THE AFTERNOON
1211 OCEAN BOULEVARD
OCEANSIDE HARBOR
LA JOLLA, CALIFORNIA
RECEPTION TO FOLLOW

(TIP)
MAIL FINISHED INVITATION IN A CLEAR TUBE

TRADITIONAL SENDOFF

THROW RICE FROM A DECORATIVE, VINTAGE-SHAPED BOX

RICE FAVORS BY JULIE TURNER

(TIP)
HANG BOXED FAVORS FROM BACK
OF GUESTS' CHAIRS

FLOWER GIRL FINERY

HANDMADE TOUCHES FOR THE TINIEST WEDDING PARTY MEMBER

FLOWER GIRL BASKET AND SHOES BY JULIE TURNER

(TIP)
CALLIGRAPHY FLOWER GIRL'S NAME OR
A SIMPLE QUOTE ONTO BOTTOM OF BASKET

DECOUPAGE DETAILS
ENHANCE METAL AND PAPER COMBINATION WITH A GLOSSY FINISH

ELEGANT WEDDING BY JAYME SHEPHERD

Brayden Shepherd
Table 10

(TIP)
MEASURE METAL SURFACE AREA BEFORE
ADHERING COAT OF DECOUPAGE TO PAPER

ELEGANT INVITATION
UNIQUE USE OF THIN SHEET METAL

WEDDING INVITATION BY JAYME SHEPHERD

(TIP)
ADD A TOUCH OF SCALLOP-EDGED
PAPER, DOTTED WITH MINI HOLES

Max & Chelsea

3
BABY

BLOOM AND GROW

POP-UP FLOWERS AND FRINGED GRASS FORM AN INVITING INVITATION

BABY SHOWER INVITATION AND LETTER ACCENT BY JOANNA BOLICK

(TIP)
CREATE A TEMPLATE OF CARD DESIGN FIRST, THEN
MODIFY USING VARIOUS PATTERNS AND COLORS

HEAD TABLE

ACCENTUATE GUEST OF HONOR'S SEATING PLACE WITH THEMED PIECES

BABY SHOWER CENTERPIECE BY JOANNA BOLICK

(TIP)

USE A PAPER SHREDDER FOR QUICK AND EASY CENTERPIECE GRASS AND STEMS

BABY KUDOS
CIRCLES FRAME METAL LETTERS

CONGRATS BY MAGGIE HOLMES

(TIP)
USE DIMENSIONAL ADHESIVE UNDER STAR FOR A 3-D LOOK

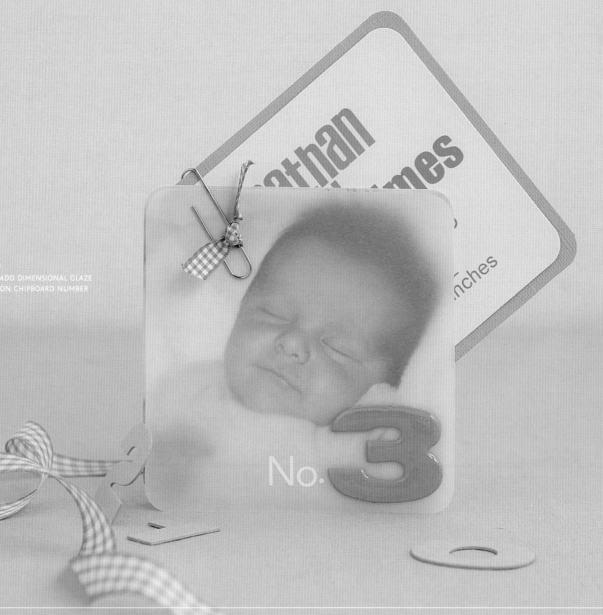

(TIP)
ADD DIMENSIONAL GLAZE
ON CHIPBOARD NUMBER

No. 3

INTERACTIVE ARRIVAL

SHOW OFF BABY WITH AS MANY PHOTO INSERTS AS YOU WISH

IT'S A GIRL BY LYNNE MONTGOMERY

(TIP)
ADD OR SUBTRACT EMBELLISHMENTS DEPENDING ON QUANTITY MADE

BUILDING BLOCKS
CUSTOM PHOTO CUBES CREATE UNIQUE NURSERY DECORATIONS

BABY GARLAND BY LYNNE MONTGOMERY

(TIP)

AFTER THREADING WITH RIBBON, SIMPLY TAPE UP
OPENINGS AND COVER WITH PHOTOS

FIRST YEAR
RECORD MONTH-TO-MONTH MILESTONES

BABY JOURNAL BY KRIS STANGER

(TIP)
ADD PHOTOS, HIGHLIGHTS AND REFLECTIONS
FOR EACH MONTH OF BABY'S FIRST YEAR

IT'S a BOY!

(TIP)
ACCENT GREEN BUTTONS WITH THREAD
AND LEAVE BLUE BUTTONS PLAIN

SUSPENDED SNAPSHOTS
MONOGRAMMED GIFTS AS UNIQUE AS THE NEW ARRIVAL

MONOGRAM PHOTO DÉCOR BY VICKI BOUTIN

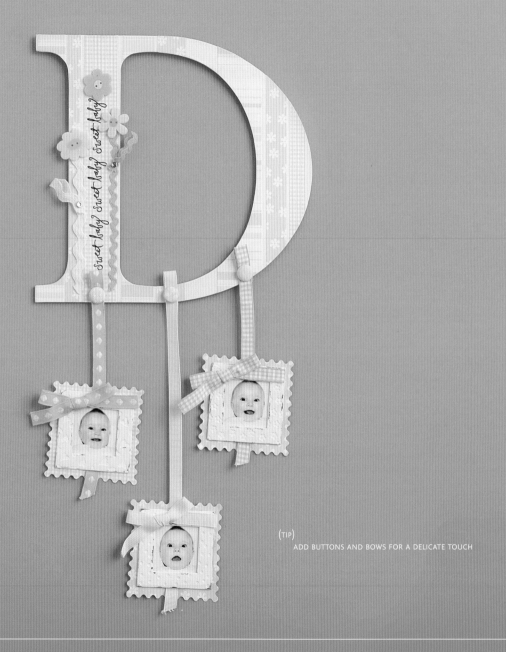

(TIP)
ADD BUTTONS AND BOWS FOR A DELICATE TOUCH

AERIAL ARTISTRY

SUSPEND FRAMED PHOTOS FOR A WHIMSICAL NURSERY MOBILE

NURSERY MOBILE BY VICKI BOUTIN

(TIP)

PAINT METAL FRAMES TO SOFTEN LOOK FOR BABY

SWEETEST THING

LIMIT COLOR PALETTE FOR A CONTROLLED LOOK

BABY SHOWER INVITE AND DÉCOR BY SHERELLE CHRISTENSEN

You're invited to a

BABY SHOWER

In honor of Lily Sheri Christensen

Daughter of David & Sherelle Christensen

On Saturday, October 15th

At 2:00 pm @ Sheri's Home

(TIP)
CUT WORDS INTO STRIPS, PLACE ON TOP
OF LEDGER PAPER AND SEW ONE SIDE

GROWN WITH LOVE

APPLY STRIPS OF COLOR AND WORDS

BABY SHOWER LAYOUT BY SHERELLE CHRISTENSEN

Lily Sheri Christensen

SWEET BABY

Precious Little Angel...

Snuggle Bug

Daddy's Little Girl

Sweet Baby Girl...Sweet Baby Girl...Sweet Baby Girl...Sweet Baby Girl...Sweet Baby Girl...Sweet Baby Girl...Sweet Baby Girl...Sweet Baby Girl...Sweet Baby Girl...

(TIP)
EMBELLISH WITH GIRLISH GOODIES

WOODEN HANGERS

CUSTOM PAINTED, EMBELLISHED AND PERSONALIZED

BABY HANGERS BY KRIS STANGER

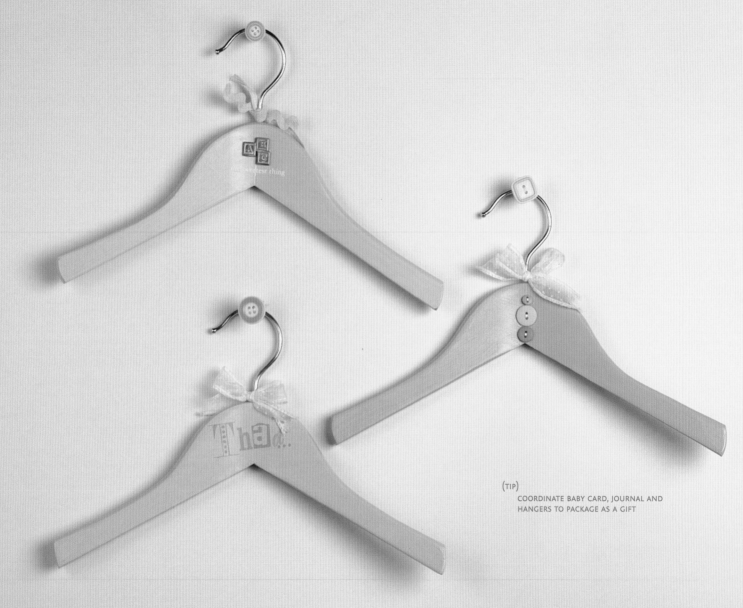

(TIP)

COORDINATE BABY CARD, JOURNAL AND
HANGERS TO PACKAGE AS A GIFT

PENNANT INVITATIONS
FUN AND EASY BABY INVITATION USING SHISH KEBAB STICKS
BABY SHOWER INVITATION AND FAVOR BAGS BY JESSICA KOPP AND MARGIE ROMNEY–ASLETT

BABY SHOWER FOR YOSHA
wednesday, JUNE 7
4-5 PM, MM creative room

IT'S A BOY!

we LOVE YOSHa!

(TIP)
CUT OUT END TRIANGLE ONLY AFTER YOU'VE
FOLDED AND SECURED IT TO STICK

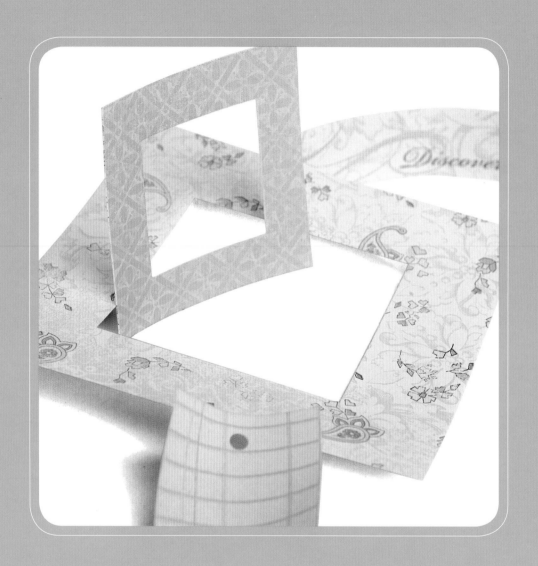

4

JANUARY
FEBRUARY

MIDNIGHT MADNESS
TAG MAKER RIMS CREATE MEMORABLE CARDS
NEW YEAR'S PARTY CARD BY CHRISTY TOMLINSON

(TIP)
EXPERIMENT WITH OTHER ITEMS IN
TAG MAKER, LIKE EPOXY STICKERS

SWIZZLE STICKS
RING IN THE NEW YEAR WITH PATTERNED CARDSTOCK FAVORS

NEW YEAR'S PARTY FAVORS BY CHRISTY TOMLINSON

(TIP)

USE A HEAVY-WEIGHT PATTERNED
PAPER TO CREATE FAVORS

KICK OFF DÉCOR
TEAM COLORS, METALLIC PAPERS AND
WIDE RIBBON ARE A WINNING COMBINATION

SUPER BOWL BASH BETTING GRID BY ROBYN WERLICH

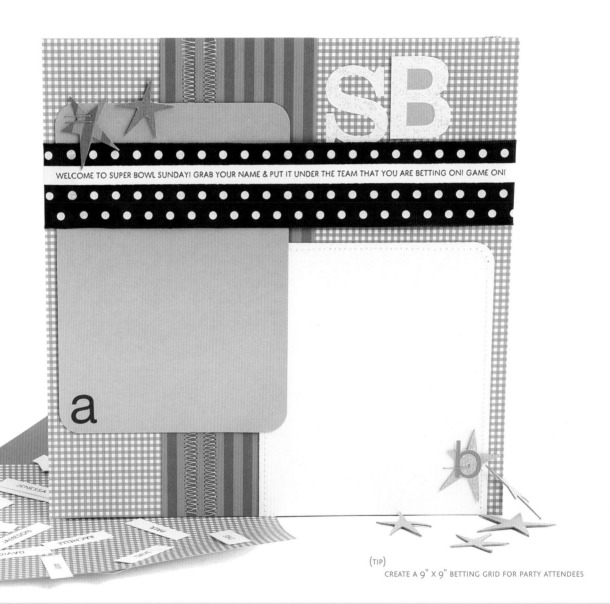

WELCOME TO SUPER BOWL SUNDAY! GRAB YOUR NAME & PUT IT UNDER THE TEAM THAT YOU ARE BETTING ON! GAME ON!

(TIP)
CREATE A 9" X 9" BETTING GRID FOR PARTY ATTENDEES

FILL 'ER UP

VELVET SAYINGS SPICE UP AN AVERAGE PITCHER

SUPER BOWL BASH PITCHER AND INVITATION BY ROBYN WERLICH

(TIP)
EMBELLISH INSTANTLY WITH RIBBON AND THREAD

SUPER BOWL SUNDAY SUPER BOWL SUNDAY SUPER BOWL SUNDAY SU

Come join our
Super Bowl Bash!

Sunday at 3 p.m.
February 4, 2007

- At the Werlich home -

Be prepared to place your bets,
cheer and have lots of fun
with friends and family!

Please bring a salad or dessert to share.

HEART TO HEART
MULTIPLY LAYERS FOR DEPTH AND DISTINCTION
VALENTINE DECORATION BY VICKI BOUTIN

(TIP)
INTERCHANGE NOTIONS AND WORDS FOR A VARIED APPEARANCE

LOVE LIGHT

ILLUMINATE JIGSAW SHAPES WITH CHRISTMAS LIGHTS

L O V E BY JIHAE KWON

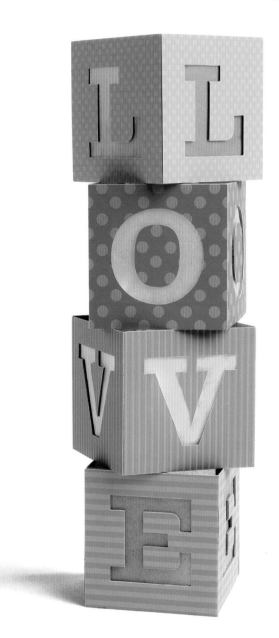

(TIP)
> SPRAY MOUNT PATTERNED PAPER
> ONTO PLAIN JIGSAW SHAPES

BLOSSOMING AFFECTION
VALENTINE CARDS, HANDMADE WITH LOVE

LOVE BLOSSOMS BY ERIN TERRELL

(TIP)
CREATE FLOWERS OUT OF GAMEBOARD HEART SHAPES

POSTAL SERVICE
CREATE A CUSTOM BOX FOR LOVE NOTES
LOVE NOTES BOX BY ERIN TERRELL

(TIP)
COVER AN ORDINARY BOX WITH BEAUTIFUL
PATTERNED PAPERS FOR CLASS VALENTINE SWAPS

VIBRANT VALENTINE
ANYTHING BUT CLASSIC PATTERNS AND DETAILS

SWEETHEART AND BE MINE CARDS BY MELLETTE BEREZOSKI

(TIP)
ADD A LITTLE FORMALITY TO CONTEMPORARY
CARDS BY WRAPPING IN VINTAGE HIP TRIMS

SWEET NOTHINGS

WRAP CANDY BARS IN COORDINATING PAPERS FOR A DELICIOUS OFFERING

9 REASONS BY MELLETTE BEREZOSKI

(TIP)
ADHERE JOURNALING STRIPS AND NUMBER
STICKERS TO EACH BAR OF CANDY

reasons why i
love you so much

5

MARCH
APRIL

FLOWERING DESSERT

PAPER FLOWERS MAKE THIS CAKE COLORFUL AND UNIQUE

BLOSSOMS CAKE BY MAGGIE HOLMES

(TIP)

INSERT BRADS THROUGH FLOWERS, LEAVING
PRONGS CLOSED, AND PLACE RIGHT INTO CAKE

BRANCH OUT

ATTACH FABRIC AND PAPER FLOWERS IN LAYERS OR ALONE

SPRING BRANCHES BY MAGGIE HOLMES

(TIP)
SPRAY PAINT ORDINARY BRANCHES WHITE

EASTER COLLAGE

COMBINE BLOCKS OF PHOTOS, PATTERNED PAPERS AND EMBELLISHMENTS

SO MANY EGGS BY MELLETTE BEREZOSKI

so many...

eggs

...so little time

HAPPY EASTER

celebrate

enjoy

We had my family over for Easter this year. We spread dozens and dozens of eggs all over the back yard. It was so much fun watching the kids race around the trees looking for eggs. Later, we grilled hamburgers and sat around the bonfire talking, laughing, and telling stories. **Such good times.**
04.15.2006

(TIP) ADD BLACK AND WHITE PHOTOS TO PREVENT BRIGHT COLORS FROM OVERWHELMING

EMBELLISHED EGGS

SCRAPBOOK ACCENTS TURN REGULAR EGGS INTO LITTLE WORKS OF ART

DECORATIVE EASTER EGGS BY MELLETTE BEREZOSKI

(TIP)
ADDING A TABLESPOON OF WHITE VINEGAR
TO DYE MIXTURE HELPS EGGS ABSORB COLOR

BLOOMING GARDEN
CONVERT PATTERNED PAPER AND EMBELLISHMENTS INTO CUSTOMIZED SEED PACKETS

GARDEN SEED PACKETS BY CHRISTY TOMLINSON

(TIP)
CAREFULLY UNDO SEAMS OF EXISTING
SEED PACKET AND USE AS TEMPLATE

POTTED ART
PAINT, DISTRESS AND DECORATE CLAY POTS
GARDEN POTS BY CHRISTY TOMLINSON

(TIP)
BEFORE PAINTING, CHIP OFF BITS
OF CLAY POT WITH HAMMER

SHAMROCK TAG

METAL-RIMMED TAGS TAKE ON A NEW SEASONAL IDENTITY

ST. PADDY'S DAY CARD BY VICKI BOUTIN

(TIP)
GROUP HEART-SHAPED TAGS
TOGETHER, FORMING A SHAMROCK

GREEN WITH ENVY
TRANSFORM RIBBON AND EMBELLISHMENTS
INTO NOVEL ACCESSORIES

ST. PADDY'S DAY BROOCH AND ACCESSORIES BY VICKI BOUTIN

lucky Me

(TIP)
PATTERNED PAPER ADDS COLOR AND INTEREST

6
MAY
JUNE

BRAG BOX
ALTERED LUNCH TINS ORGANIZE LOOSE PHOTOS

GRANDMA'S BRAG BOX BY LYNNE MONTGOMERY

(TIP)
USE SCRAP CARDSTOCK AS A TEMPLATE
FOR CUTTING PATTERNED PAPER

Happy Mother's Day

(TIP)
MAKE SURE SEWN STRIPS ARE WIDE ENOUGH
TO ACCOMMODATE A GOOD GRIP FOR TEARING

FAMILY TIES
SHADOWBOXES BECOME INTERACTIVE
MY FAMILY BY GAIL PIERCE-WATNE

(TIP)
ADD NUMEROUS PAGES TO SHADOWBOX
BY ATTACHING BINDER RINGS AT BASE

MEMORIES FOR MOM

QUICK AND EASY ALBUM LETS HER KNOW SHE IS LOVED

MOTHER'S DAY ALBUM BY SHERELLE CHRISTENSEN

(TIP)

MINI ALBUMS MAKE IT SIMPLE TO PUT
TOGETHER BEAUTIFUL, FUNCTIONAL RECORDS

HIS TIME

PUT MASCULINE COLORS AND ACCENTS TO GOOD USE

FATHER'S DAY CARDS BY MELLETTE BEREZOSKI

(TIP)

PRINT JOURNALING ON WHITE CARDSTOCK
AND USE AS A BACKDROP

If I could do this again, I'd just work harder to be quiet, open to songs in all the keys of life. My kids didn't have a perfect father. My bet is yours won't either. But they won't need one - not as long as they've got you. ~ Hugh O'Neill

memories

SMART · UNIQUE · STRONG

cherish

Heritage
journey

miss you
a legacy of love

Edward Lee Berezoski
1918~1977

(TIP)
USE TAG MAKER TO FRAME SMALL PHOTOS
AND UNIFY ROUND ACCENTS ON BOARD

COME TOGETHER

COMBINE BRIGHT, COMPLEMENTARY COLORS

CHANG FAMILY REUNION INVITATION AND COASTERS BY JIHAE KWON

(TIP)

BOLD, SIMPLISTIC COLORS TIE COORDINATED PIECES TOGETHER

張

FAMILY REUNION

LAS VEGAS NEVADA
JUNE 2006

PRESERVE THE MEMORIES
CHANGE BOX APPEARANCE WITH COLORFUL CARDSTOCK

CHANG FAMILY REUNION KEEPSAKE BOX BY JIHAE KWON

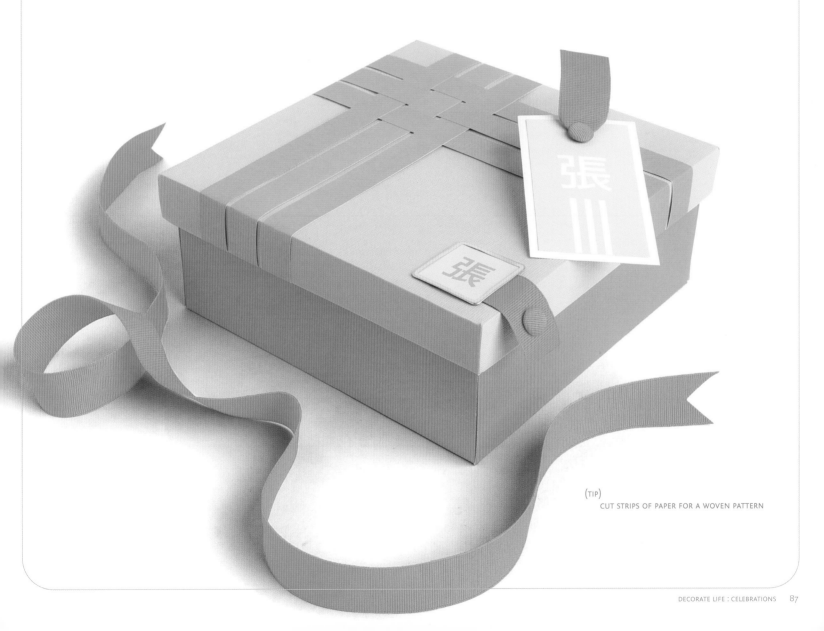

(TIP)
CUT STRIPS OF PAPER FOR A WOVEN PATTERN

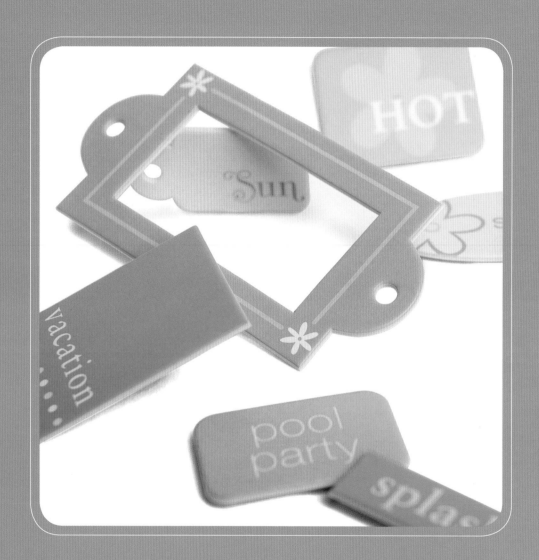

7
JULY · AUGUST
SEPTEMBER

STAR SPANGLED

CREATE AN INTERESTING OVERLAY WITH VELLUM AND CHIPBOARD SHAPES

4TH OF JULY BY MAGGIE HOLMES

come
celebrate the

4th
Of
JULy

with the Wilson Family.

& fun!

the party begins at
5:00pm sharp
in our backyard.
see you then!

(TIP)
COAT STARS WITH SILVER PAINT,
THEN AGAIN WITH GLITTER PAINT

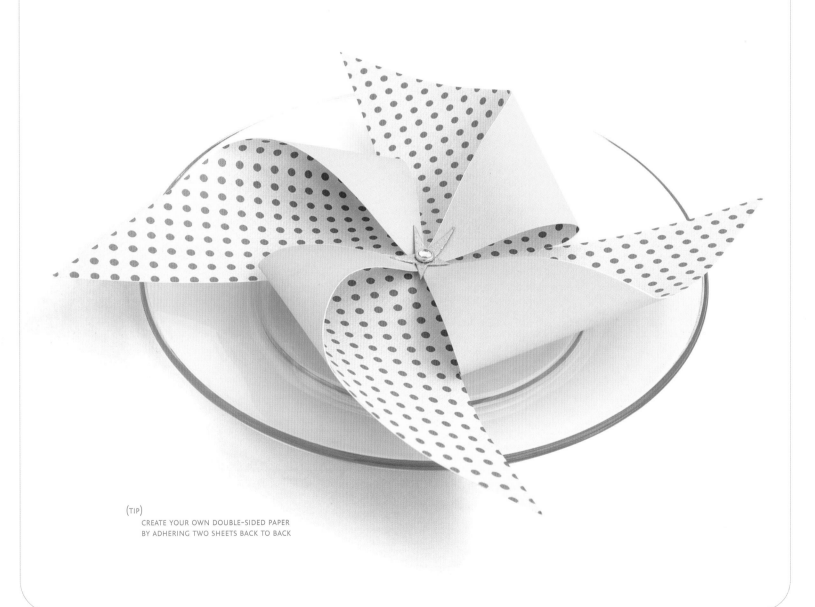

(TIP)

CREATE YOUR OWN DOUBLE-SIDED PAPER
BY ADHERING TWO SHEETS BACK TO BACK

FLIP OUT

MAKE A VASE FOR STAMPED FLOWERS
OUT OF EMBELLISHED FLIP FLOPS

FLIP FLOP CENTERPIECE BY MELLETTE BEREZOSKI

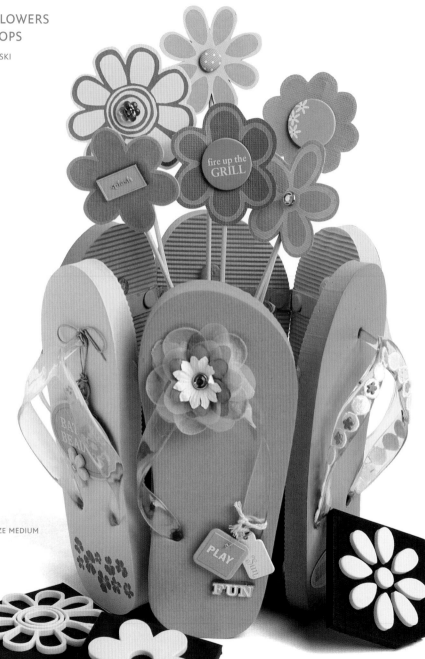

(TIP)

USE THREE SETS OF FLIP FLOPS IN A CHILD'S SIZE MEDIUM

MAKE A SPLASH

SUMMER-THEMED DETAILS KEEP THIS CARD COOL AND FESTIVE

POOL PARTY INVITATION BY MELLETTE BEREZOSKI

(TIP)
SLIDE BAND ON AND OFF BY
WRAPPING CARD FIRST WITH
VELLUM, THEN WITH RIBBON

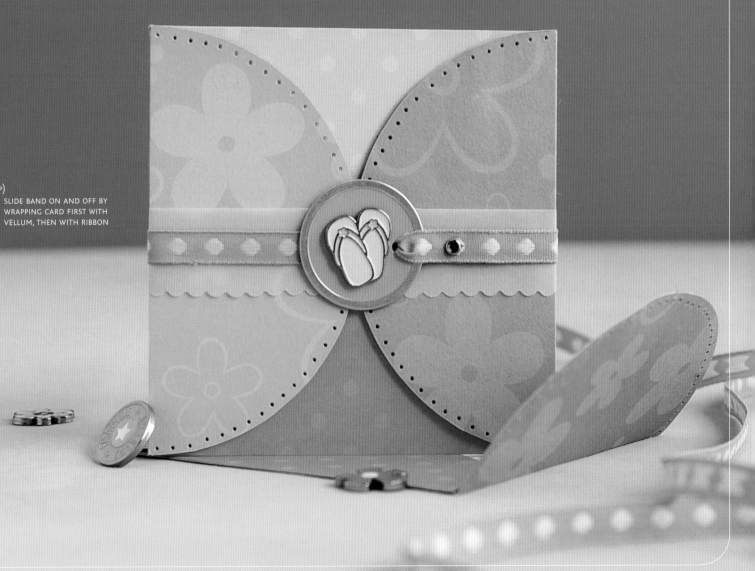

TEAM ROSTER

LAYOUT UNFOLDS TO REVEAL PLAYERS

SUMMER PARTY DÉCOR COLLAGE BY KRIS STANGER

(TIP)

TAKE A QUICK SNAPSHOT OF EACH
TEAMMATE AT PRACTICE, RESULTING IN
A GREAT COACH'S GIFT AT SEASON'S END

(TIP)
ADD FISHING LINE TO ENDS FOR EXTRA HANGING LENGTH

LIGHT SHADES

COORDINATING SHADES ADD SPARKLE TO OUTDOOR PARTIES

PARTY LIGHTS BY JULIE TURNER

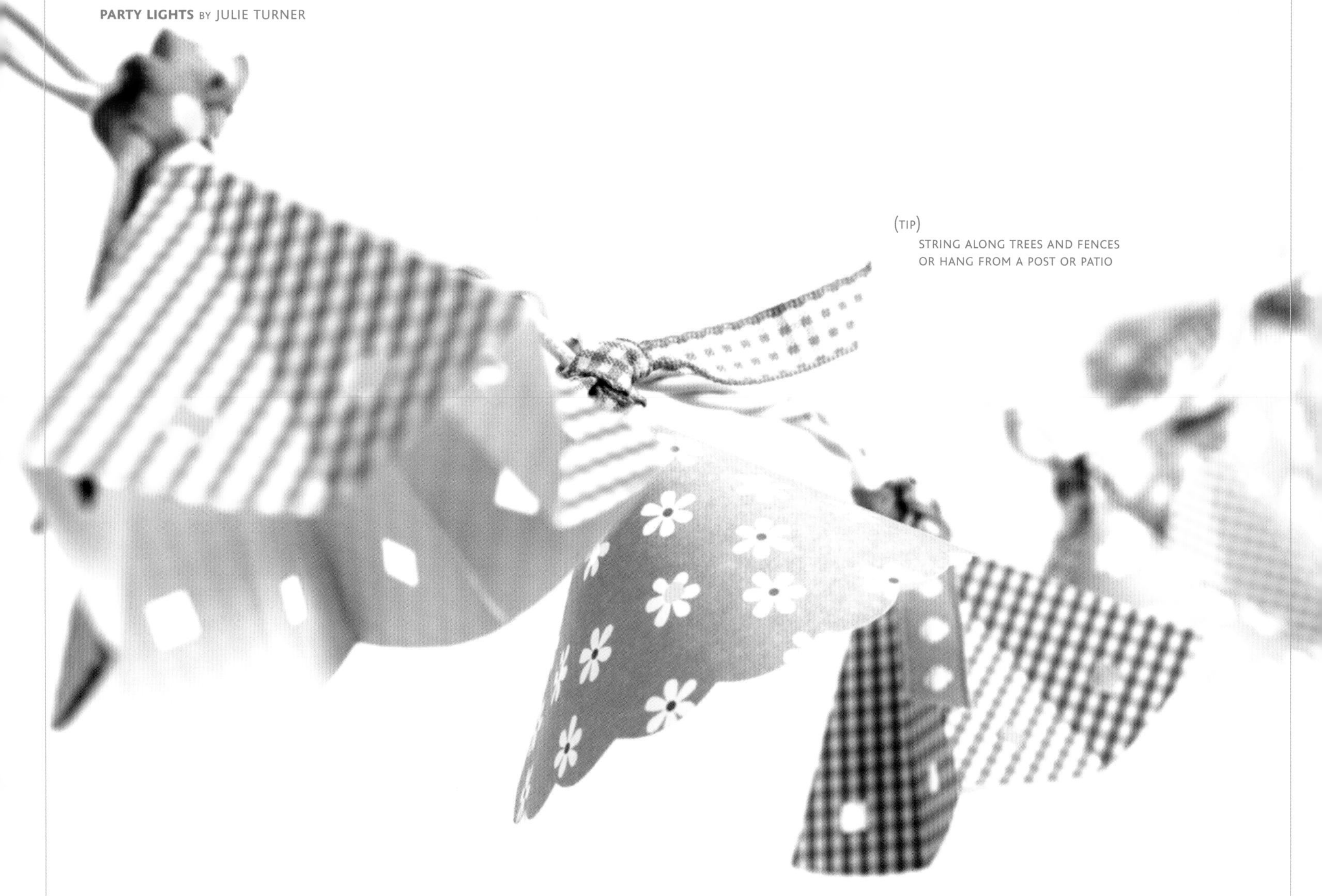

(TIP)
STRING ALONG TREES AND FENCES
OR HANG FROM A POST OR PATIO

GARDEN PARTY
ENLIVEN OUTDOOR PARTIES WITH STAMPED NAPKINS AND MATCHING CUPCAKE TOPPERS
GARDEN PARTY INVITATION AND DECORATION BY JULIE TURNER

please join us for a

garden
party

saturday, july 14
6:30 p.m.
2054 east rose lane
gilbert, arizona

r.s.v.p. 555-1234

(TIP)
USE A HEAT-SETTING PIGMENT INK WHEN STAMPING NAPKINS

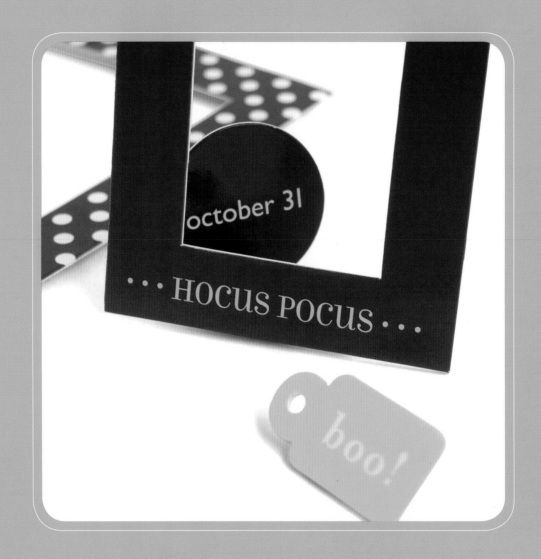

8
OCTOBER
NOVEMBER

GHOULISH GREETINGS
PRINT PARTY DETAILS ON A TRANSPARENCY AND LAYER OVER CARDSTOCK

BOO BY MAGGIE HOLMES

trick or treat

BOO

Spooky fun
scary
halloween party
at Tyler's house
October 31st, 2006
5:00 - 9:00pm
Prizes will be awarded
for best costumes!

(TIP)
USE ADHESIVE FROM COLORBOARD STICKER AS TAG

(TIP)
PUNCH HOLES IN ORANGE CARDSTOCK,
THEN LAYER OVER BLACK PATTERNED PAPER

LURID LAYOUT
SHOWCASE HALLOWEEN THROUGH THE YEARS

BOO SCRAPBOOK LAYOUT AND CANDY BAG BY ERIN TERRELL

(TIP)
ADD ENVELOPES TO HOLD EXTRA PHOTOS,
JOURNALING OR MEMORABILIA

TRICK AND TREAT

SMALL BUCKETS FILLED WITH CANDY MAKE GREAT FAVORS FOR GUESTS

BOO INVITATION AND CANDY DISHES BY ERIN TERRELL

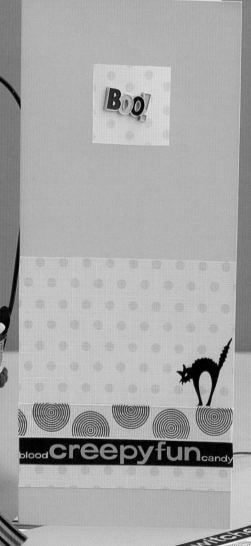

(TIP)
WRITE NAMES ON BUCKETS AFTER
COVERING WITH CHALKBOARD PAINT

SPINE-CHILLING DINING

COORDINATE RUB-ONS, RIBBON AND PAPER
FOR A COMPLETE PLACE SETTING

HALLOWEEN PLACE SETTING BY CHRISTY TOMLINSON

(TIP)

USE A CHARGER INSTEAD OF A PLATE
LEAVING MORE ROOM FOR RUB-ONS

CANDY COLLAGE

CREATE A WORD MONTAGE WITH VARYING RUB-ON SIZES AND COLORS

HALLOWEEN CANDY VASE BY CHRISTY TOMLINSON

(TIP)

USE RUB-ON COLORS THAT CONTRAST WITH VASE FILLING

GIVING TRAY

PHOTOS OF PAST THANKSGIVING CELEBRATIONS DECORATE SERVING TRAY

GIVE THANKS TRAY BY ERIN TERRELL

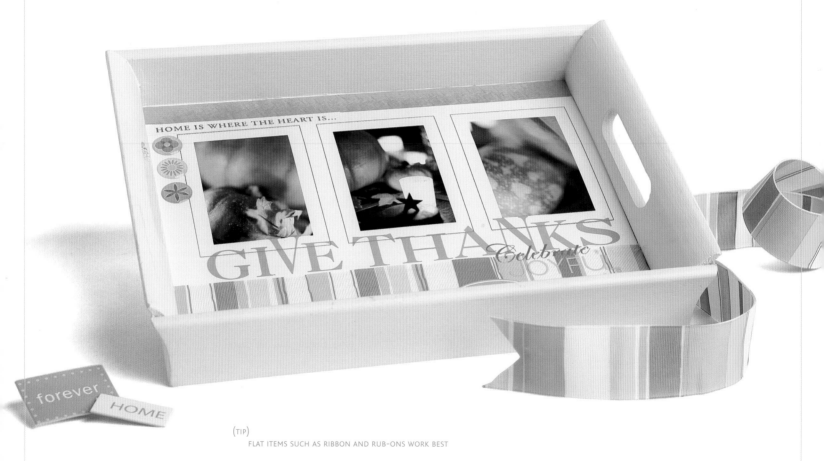

(TIP)

FLAT ITEMS SUCH AS RIBBON AND RUB-ONS WORK BEST

(TIP)

KEEP THINGS FRESH BY SEASONALLY
SELECTING NEW PHOTOS

9
DECEMBER

JOYFUL TIDINGS
SEND COLORFUL CHRISTMAS CARDS TO BRIGHTEN THE HOLIDAYS

JOY CARD SET BY ERIN TERRELL

(TIP)
CREATE FAST CARDS DURING THE BUSY SEASON
WITH MATCHING PAPER AND STICKER SETS

JOY

JOY

MERRY CHRISTMAS

HAPPY HOLIDAYS
USE A CIRCLE PUNCH TO CREATE EASY-TO-DUPLICATE CARDS

TREE CARD SET BY ERIN TERRELL

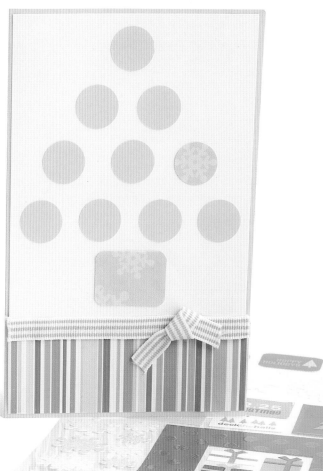

(TIP)
BOLD, COORDINATING PAPERS MAKE A WHIMSICAL SET OF CARDS

SEASONS GREETINGS

TRANSPARENCIES PRODUCE A UNIQUE, FLOATING EFFECT

HAPPY HOLIDAYS BY MAGGIE HOLMES

(TIP)

USE AN EMBOSSING TEMPLATE OR FOAM STAMP
TO CONSTRUCT POLKA DOT EFFECT

STILL FRAME

TAKE PICTURES OF CHRISTMAS ORNAMENTS FOR USE ON GREETING CARDS

HOLIDAY CARDS BY MAGGIE HOLMES

may your days be merry and bright

we wish you peace joy and love

(TIP)
COVER CHIPBOARD WITH A COMBINATION OF PATTERNED PAPER
AND DIAMOND GLAZE OR BEADS AND DIAMOND GLAZE

SHEER DELIGHT

GIVE TRADITIONAL CARDS A CONTEMPORARY SPIN
WITH SHEER FRAMES AND PLEXIGLAS

SHEER CHRISTMAS CARDS BY MELLETTE BEREZOSKI

(TIP)
ADHERE COORDINATING PAPER TO BACK OF
PLEXIGLAS FOR A PLACE TO WRITE SENTIMENTS

CLEARLY SPECIAL
PLEASE NEIGHBORS WITH A PICTURE PERFECT OFFERING

FROM OUR HOME TO YOURS BY MELLETTE BEREZOSKI

(TIP)
AVOID SCRATCHING PHOTO INSIDE ORNAMENT BY ATTACHING
A PIECE OF PAPER TOWEL TO ENDS OF TWEEZERS

HANGING FRAMES

SHAPED EYELET CHARMS BECOME DECORATIVE HANGING HOOKS

PEACE, LOVE AND JOY BY JENNIFER JENSEN

(TIP)
PLACE ON TREE, HANG FROM GARLAND
OR SEND TO GRANDPARENTS

RUFFLED RIBBON

LAYER AND GATHER RIBBON FOR A DECORATIVE BORDER

CHLOE AND MIA BY JENNIFER JENSEN

(TIP)
USE LIQUID ADHESIVE TO GATHER RIBBON

CENTER PIECE
HARMONIOUS TABLE DECORATION FOR HOLIDAY PARTIES

HOLIDAY CENTERPIECE BY JOANNA BOLICK

(TIP)
USE GLUE DOTS TO ADHERE
EMBELLISHMENTS TO WREATH

PAPER STOCKINGS
ADORN YOUR MANTLE WITH THIS SIMPLE, HANDMADE ACCENT

CHRISTMAS STOCKINGS BY JOANNA BOLICK

(TIP)
CREATE YOUR OWN STOCKING PATTERN
OR DOWNLOAD ONE FROM THE INTERNET

SWEET AND SIMPLE

TREAT YOUR NEIGHBORS WITH THIS TASTEFUL COMBINATION

NEIGHBOR GIFTS BY JENNY WESTON

merrychristmas

(TIP)
USING DECORATIVE SCISSORS CAN
CHANGE THE ENTIRE LOOK OF A CARD

merry Christmas

(TIP)
COMBINE BOTH TRADITIONAL AND NON-TRADITIONAL
HOLIDAY MATERIALS FOR AN ECLECTIC EFFECT

DECORATIVE DISPLAY

PAINTED CANVAS AND POCKETS PRESENT HOLIDAY CARDS
IN AN EYE-CATCHING WAY

CHRISTMAS CARD HOLDER BY CHRISTY TOMLINSON

(TIP)

PRE-SEW CARDSTOCK STRIPS BEFORE ADHERING TO CANVAS

NOEL, NOEL
PAINT AND COVER PINE BLOCKS
WITH PATTERNED PAPER AND EMBELLISHMENTS

CHRISTMAS BLOCKS BY CHRISTY TOMLINSON

(TIP)
PAINT LIGHTLY FOR A VINTAGE APPEARANCE

10
BOOK END

PAGE 10 - 11 MARGIE ROMNEY-ASLETT

GIRLFRIENDS LUNCH INVITE

1. Using mod podge and a foam brush, cover jigsaw alphabet of guest's initials
2. Pour shimmer on top, let dry and tap

GIRLFRIENDS LUNCH FAVORS

1. Stamp metal rimmed tags
2. Use tiny alphas and hand stamp for information

Printed paper, MM kids trims (kate), league paper, cheeky jigsaw alphabet, metal rimmed tags, crystal brads, magnetic stamp, ink, clearly defined, shimmer and tiny alphas: Making Memories

Bottles: Container Store

Glossy decoupage: Mod Podge by Plaid

Other: soap

PAGES 12 - 13 MELLETTE BEREZOSKI

I COULD NOT LOVE YOU MORE

1. Round corners on blue background cardstock
2. Cut a 10¾" x 1¾" piece of white cardstock and attach to center of blue background
3. Computer print title, journaling and decorative brushes on solid cardstock and attach to page
4. Machine stitch around photo and attach to page above title
5. Create a matte for large number by stitching together dots paper and solid orange cardstock
6. Attach number with foam tape for added dimension
7. Finish off with stripe paper border, ribbons, ribbon label and ribbon button

MM kids paper and trims (max), vintage hip paper (paisley), scallop edged cardstock paper (childhood), textured cardstock paper (cityscape), nothing but numbers (in bloom), ribbon label and ribbon brads: Making Memories

Computer font: MS Reference Serif, Microsoft Word and Euphorigenic from dafont.com

Digital brushes: Rhonna Swirls from twopeasinabucket.com

FIVE

1. Cut a 4¼" x 5½" piece of orange cardstock, rounding off corners
2. Cut a 3⅞" x 5⅛" piece of dots paper and adhere to orange cardstock
3. Print party information on vellum and trim to fit over dots paper
4. Spell out age by applying appropriate stickers to blue cardstock and trim excess paper
5. Punch circle on one end of blue cardstock and attach over vellum

6. Add washer and medium brad inside punched circle
7. Cut a narrow strip of darker blue cardstock and adhere below stickers

MM kids paper (max), vintage hip paper (paisley), nothing but numbers (in bloom), washer words and medium brads: Making Memories

Circle punch: Marvy Uchida

Font: Typo Latin Serif and Euphorigenic from dafont.com

Other: vellum

FIRE-CRACKER FAVORS

1. Cut a 9½" x 24" piece of tissue paper
2. Tape one end of tissue paper to an empty toilet paper roll, wrap completely around and tape other end down
3. Gather tissue paper on one end of roll and tie with string
4. Fill with candy, stickers and small toys through open end of roll
5. Gather and tie up open end of roll
6. Cut a 4½" x 6" piece of patterned paper and adhere to center part of roll
7. Wrap ribbon around roll and finish with page pebble

MM kids paper and trims (max), felt ribbon and page pebbles (thank you): Making Memories

Other: tissue paper and string

PAGES 14 - 15 ERIN TERRELL

PICTURE YOURSELF AT MY PARTY

1. Print invitation on white textured cardstock using bernhardt fashion font (internet)
2. Add mini frame to invitation and tie ribbon through it
3. Mount invitation first on pink cardstock, then on patterned paper

PICTURE YOURSELF AFTER THE PARTY CAMERA

1. Wrap camera or box by covering with patterned paper

Cardstock paper (cityscape), simply fabulous paper (maddi), trims (maddi) and jump rings: Making Memories

Other: mini frame by K&Co and Camera by Kodak

PICTURE YOURSELF AFTER THE PARTY ALBUM

1. Decorate album front with ribbon, eyelet tags, rub-ons and rhinestones
2. Cover each interior page with patterned paper
3. Add photos and photo mattes of solid cardstock
4. Add embellishments
5. Add ribbon tabs to outer edges of various pages

Simply fabulous paper (maddi) and trims (maddi), 5" x 7" mini album, label holders, staples and rub-ons: Making Memories

Other: rhinestones by Heidi Swapp

PAGE 16 - 17 ROBYN WERLICH

OUR SHINING STAR GIFT BOX

1. Using a template, cut out gift box and sew together sides, tying together with ribbon on fourth side
2. Loop wire around top for handle and add painted sticker and embellishments

OUR SHINING STAR BUCKET

1. Punch small circles from red cardstock and attach to metal pail
2. Add cardstock and star to pixie stick and finish with rub-ons

OUR SHINING STAR CARD

1. Print invitation text on cardstock, then add sewing and ribbon
2. Paint chipboard stars with blue and white ink, then brush glitter glue on top
3. Add brown strip of cardstock, stars and crystal brads

Cardstock paper (childhood and hampton), MM kids paper (sam), nothing but numbers (spotlight), gameboard shapes (stars), ribbon brads (red/denim), crystal brads (clear circle) and rub-ons mini (birthday 2): Making Memories

Barefoot professor: twopeasinabucket.com

Font: Century Gothic

Other: sewing, staples and wire

PAGE 18 - 19 JENNIFER JENSEN

PARTY INVITE

1. Cut a 5" x 10" piece of cardstock for card base
2. Cut a 3½" square of patterned cardstock for frame (can also use sticker frames)
3. With a 1¾" square punch, remove center of frame for windowed opening
4. Trim photo and paper backing to size of tag
5. Sandwich a 12" piece of thin ribbon or twine (folded in half) between the two and adhere
6. Place photo tag in center of frame, making sure that both ends of twine are under frame and adhere to top of card
7. Wrap loose ends around crystal brads at top of card

Cardstock paper (in bloom), boho chic paper, magnetic stamp alphabet and square tags: Making Memories

Other: jute twine

PARTY PLACEMAT

1. Place a 12" x 12" piece of cardstock onto paper trimmer, angled like a diamond and cut through center, leaving two diagonal pieces
2. Repeat step one to create a total of four triangles
3. Create frame by slightly overlapping four triangles of paper

4. Add crystal brads at each point of inside diamond to hold in place
5. Slide photo under frame and hold in place with black cardstock
6. Wrap a piece of ribbon around envelope and tuck flap under right side of placemat, leaving room for utensils
7. Leave blank paper in envelope for guests to write a birthday note

Boho chic paper, crystal brads, magnetic stamp ornaments and envelope (in bloom): Making Memories

Other: ribbon

PAGE 20 - 21 MAGGIE HOLMES

SHH . . .

1. Cut two pieces of cardstock and adhere wrong sides together, only on edges
2. Use rub-ons to spell 'shh . . .' across front of card
3. Use sewing machine to stitch two lines across card, creating a pocket
4. Use a circle punch to remove a half circle at end of pocket
5. Print party details on strip of paper, cut to fit in pocket
6. Add paper flowers to end of pull-out, insert into pocket and round corners

Patterned paper, rub-ons, mini blossoms and brads: Making Memories

Corner rounder: Creative Memories

Font: Big Caslon

Other: sewing machine, thread and circle punch

MENU AND PLACE CARD

1. Type menu and matte with patterned paper
2. Round corners
3. Cut rectangles of cardstock for place cards and matte with alternating color
4. Use rub-ons to spell out names
5. Tape ribbon to back of name card
6. Attach mini blossoms with brads

Patterned paper, rub-ons, mini blossoms and brads: Making Memories

Corner rounder: Creative Memories

Font: Baskerville

PAGE 22 - 23 ROBYN WERLICH

CELEBRATE MONOGRAM LETTER

1. Cover monogram letter with ledger paper
2. Print 'celebrate' numerous times on ledger paper, cut strip and add to letter with brads and embellishments

CELEBRATE CARD

1. Cut a 5" x 10" piece of ledger paper for card
2. Wrap brown cardstock completely around card to create a closure
3. Add strips of paper, and 'celebrate' text to metal-edged tag and thread to close

CELEBRATE FAVOR BOXES

1. Cover one side of favor boxes with cardstock
2. Add rub-ons, metal charm and thread to embellish

Boho chic paper, vintage hip paper, tag maker rims, ledger paper and charmed words: Making Memories

PAGES 26 - 27 MELLETTE BEREZOSKI

BRIDAL SHOWER INVITATION

1. Cut an 8½" x 9½" piece of plum cardstock
2. Fold each end 2⅛" toward the middle, using bone folder to crease
3. Round top corner of each flap
4. Adhere boho chic paper to front flaps, trimming off excess paper
5. Print party information and apply decorative rub-ons to a piece of 3⅞" x 9⅛" white cardstock
6. Attach white cardstock to inside of card
7. Wrap sheer ribbon around middle of card and top with petals and boho chic brad accent

Boho chic paper and brad accents (lauren), petals (spotlight) and textured cardstock paper (in bloom): Making Memories

Font: Modern No. 20 and Chopin Script from dafont.com

Decorative rub-ons: Autumn Leaves

Sheer ribbon: Michaels

BRIDAL SHOWER FAVOR BOXES

1. Cut a 6" x 6" piece of patterned paper
2. Fold all four corners to center, using bone folder to crease
3. Fold all four corners again to center, using bone folder to crease
4. Unfold and place small gift in center
5. Refold paper, covering up gift
6. Tie sheer ribbon around favor box and top with tiny blossoms

Boho chic paper (lauren), mini blossoms and bone folder: Making Memories

Sheer ribbon: Michaels

JULIE AND ALAN

1. Cut two 4¼" x 4¼" pieces of chipboard and place on flat surface next to each other
2. Attach two hinges between chipboard pieces, securing with brads
3. Turn hinged piece over to front
4. Attach a 4¼" x 4¼" photo to right chipboard piece and add blossom and brad
5. Print title on white photo paper and place behind frame sticker
6. Attach crystal brad to trim and wrap around left side of boho chic frame
7. Place title and frame sticker behind boho chic frame and attach to left chipboard piece

Boho chic frame (vignette), ephemera sticker frame, trims and brad accents (lauren), blossoms (wildflower spotlight) and hinges: Making Memories

Font: Chopin Script from dafont.com

PAGE 28 - 29 LONI STEVENS

WEDDING FAVORS

1. Sew 3" width of tulle into long casing
2. Cut tulle into 8" lengths
3. Cut plastic sheeting into pieces 3" x 3½"
4. Apply appropriate rub-ons in center
5. Put small amount of adhesive on edges of plastic and roll so it will fit into tulle tube
6. Fill with candy or nuts and tie each end with ribbon

Rub-ons mini: Making Memories

Sheer ribbon: Michaels

Other: tulle and plastic sheeting

WEDDING INVITATION

1. Cut paper approximately 11" x 5"
2. Score paper into three panels that measure 3", 4" and 4"
3. Fold bottom 4" panel up and cover with paper
4. On 3" top panel, emboss design using circle template
5. Create greeting and adhere to bottom inch of top panel
6. Embellish with mini blossom and gems
7. Round corners, then use slot punch to create fold in bottom panel for tuck closure and embellish with brad

MM kids paper (ethan), mini blossoms (pink mix), simply fabulous gem stickers (clear), brads and cardstock paper: Making Memories

PAGE 30 - 31 JULIE TURNER

PAINTED BUD VASE

1. Pour a few teaspoons of paint into a glass bud vase and swirl around until inside is completely covered
2. Drain out all excess paint, making sure no puddles are left on bottom
3. Leave plenty of drying time (it can take a week or more) or use a blow-dryer to speed up process
4. Embellish with patterned paper and a ribbon tie that coordinates with wedding color theme
5. Don't leave water in vase for an extended period of time which can cause paint to peel away from glass
6. To prolong life of vase, use a water tube on end of flower bud or use an oil-based enamel paint

Scrapbook colors acrylic paint and simply fabulous paper and trims: Making Memories

Glass bud vases: IKEA

WEDDING GUEST BOOKS

1. Make front and back covers of accordion book by covering two pieces of chipboard with patterned paper
2. Fold plain cardstock to create a 10-panel accordion insert (two pieces of paper may need to be glued together to get that length) and adhere it to inside of front and back covers
3. Attach a coin envelope to each panel of accordion
4. Create envelope seals using coordinating patterned paper, a xyron sticker machine and a circle punch
5. Make simple, folded note cards with a ribbon tie embellishment to fit in envelopes
6. Keep book closed by making a paper band that can be slid on and off
7. Print the words 'guest book' on band and add a ribbon tie for embellishment

Simply fabulous paper and trims: Making Memories

Coin envelopes: Bazzill

PAGE 32 - 33 KEISHA CAMPBELL

WEDDING MEMOIR

1. Stamp flourish about 1½" from bottom of cardstock and add rhinestones
2. Cut a 1½" strip of patterned paper and glue 2" from bottom of cardstock
3. Cut ½" of patterned paper, scallop edge, then glue under first piece of paper
4. Stitch seam of two papers with zig-zag stitch
5. Cut a 6" x 6" piece of patterned paper and scallop one side, then glue to left side of project and staple top left corner
6. Add photos and a bit of machine stitching to sides of photos

7. Embellish corners of photos with blossoms and buttons
8. Adhere sticker to lower right of photo
9. Print couples names on a piece of cardstock, add bits of paint to edges and glue to project
10. Print wedding info on a tag slip under photo and stitch to project

MM kids paper (ethan), mini blossoms (pink mix), simply fabulous gem stickers (clear), brads and cardstock paper: Making Memories

BOHO WEDDING FRAME

1. Cut paper to size of frame and cut out center opening
2. Punch out die cut flowers
3. Punch hole in flower for brads or glue gem stickers in centers
4. Glue to frame
5. Using sandpaper, file edges to give a slight worn look

BOHO WEDDING CANDLE

1. Paint top of candle tin
2. Cut paper to fit side of candle tin and glue on
3. Glue ribbon to bottom candle tin top
4. Once top is dry, glue on flowers and buttons
5. Add tag

BOHO WEDDING FLOWER GIRL PAIL

1. Paint embossed flowers and leaves and let dry
2. Paint entire pail, going over flowers to tone them down (may need two coats)
3. Paint inside and handle
4. Once dry, glue ribbon to pail

Boho chic paper and trims, vintage hip paper and buttons, blossoms, simply fabulous gem stickers, ribbon and ribbon buckle, crystal brads, chipboard stickers, foam stamps and scrapbook colors acrylic paint (polo club): Making Memories

Cardstock paper and vanilla paint: Bazzill

Other: mother of pearl buttons, all night media flower punch and office supply tag

PAGE 34 - 35 JENNIFER JENSEN

LOVE CANDLE HOLDERS

1. Rub words and images onto glass, cylinder-shaped candle holders
2. Pour sand into bottom of candle holder
3. Place candle on sand and add shells
4. Drop in photo, placing on side of candle

Rub-ons alphabet (misunderstood), rub-ons images (love), rub-ons wordage (wedding) and charmed wedding: Making Memories

Glass candle holders and candles: Michaels

Other: mini jute twine

GUESTS TABLE NUMBERS

1. Dye tags to desired shade
2. Rub on table seating number
3. Take twine and string two tags together, around the top and through the two tag holes
4. Place brad through top tag only
5. Fan two tags out to set on table

Eclectic brads (beach), dyeable tags (large), scrapbook dye (evergreen), rub-ons alphabet (misunderstood) and rub-ons images (love): Making Memories

Other: mini jute twine

WEDDING INVITATION

1. Using desired font, print wedding information onto 8" square paper
2. Cut four bamboo sticks each to 11"
3. Sandwich invitation between two sticks on right and left side and adhere
4. Adhere a 12" piece of ribbon or trim under left piece of bamboo (after invite is rolled up, ribbon ties around piece)
5. Rub on decorative image and place seashell brad in center
6. Roll, tie and mail

Boho chic trims (lauren), eclectic brads (beach) and rub-ons images (love): Making Memories

Bamboo sticks: placemat from Pier1

Other: mini jute twine

Computer fonts: Felix Titling and Passions Conflict ROB

MONOGRAM FAN

1. Cut two pieces of paper to 8" x 8" and round each corner
2. Rub monogram letters in center of paper
3. Sandwich two bamboo sticks in between two papers and adhere
4. Wrap twine and ribbon in between sticks and glue
5. Place brad in center of sticks over center of wrapped twine

Eclectic brads (beach), boho chic trims and paper (lauren) and rub-ons alphabet (misunderstood): Making Memories

Bamboo sticks: placemat from Pier1

Corner rounder: Marvy

Other: mini jute twine

PAGE 36 - 37 JULIE TURNER

RICE FAVORS

1. Using patterned paper, cut, score, fold and glue favor box
2. Create handle by running ribbon through punched holes on each side of favor
3. Tie knots on inside of favor
4. Embellish with ribbon, gems, flowers and pieces of coordinated patterned paper
5. Fill with rice and a few tiny paper flowers, then seal with a sticky tab or glue dot

Vintage hip paper and trims and simply fabulous gem stickers: Making Memories

Other: paper flower

FLOWER GIRL BASKET

1. Spray paint inside and outside of an oval papier-mâché box
2. Line inner sides with patterned paper
3. Decorate outside with sticker strips, ribbon and gems
4. Attach ribbon handle through carefully punched holes

Vintage hip paper, stickers and trims and simply fabulous gem stickers: Making Memories

Spray paint: Krylon

Papier-mâché box: Michaels

FLOWER GIRL SHOES

1. Glue ribbon along each strap of mary jane-style shoes
2. Onto each strap, tie a small piece of ribbon and glue on a paper flower
3. Line inside of shoe with a patterned paper or fabric that matches flower girl basket

Vintage hip paper and trims and simply fabulous gem stickers: Making Memories

Shoes: Sam & Libby

Other: paper flowers

PAGE 38 - 39 JAYME SHEPHERD

ELEGANT WEDDING CENTER PIECE

1. Cut paper to fit around entire surface of galvanized metal bucket
2. Adhere paper to bucket using decoupage, let dry and seal outside of paper with decoupage
3. Using tag maker, crimp photo into round metal rim
4. Make small hole in side of photo tag, tie ribbon through it and attach to center of flower
5. Cut six 1" x 2" strips of tissue paper and six 1" x 1" strips to form flower
6. Fold each tissue strip in half and round off one end to make petal

7. Twist square ends of each strip around floral wire, wrap together with floral tape and finish off center of flower with decorative brad

Boho chic paper (olivia) and brad accents (lauren), tag maker and tag maker rims (circle): Making Memories

Galvanized metal bucket: Target

Glossy decoupage: Mod Podge by Plaid

Floral tape, floral wire, silk flowers and tissue paper: Michaels

ELEGANT WEDDING PLACE CARD

1. Cut a 3" x 5" rectangle out of thin sheet metal and fold in half so it can stand up on table
2. Cut piece of decorative paper to fit on side of place card, leaving a border
3. Scallop edge of top paper, add name to place card, adhere to metal using decoupage and let dry
4. Using the instant setter, punch a hole in center of each scallop for a decorative touch
5. Seal top with decoupage
6. Add flower petal with decorative brad in center

Metal sheets, scallop-edged cardstock paper (in bloom), boho chic paper and brad accent (lauren), instant setter and gem stickers: Making Memories

Glossy decoupage: Mod Podge by Plaid

Silk flower: Michaels

ELEGANT WEDDING CANDLE FAVOR

1. Cut paper to wrap around outside of metal candle container
2. Adhere to metal using decoupage, let dry, then seal with decoupage
3. Cut patterned paper to fit top of lid and adhere
4. Cut smaller circle out of photograph and adhere
5. Seal lid with decoupage
6. Add flower with decorative center

Boho chic paper and brad accents (lauren), cardstock tags and gem stickers: Making Memories

Candle and silk flower: Michaels

WEDDING INVITATION

1. For inner envelope, fold an 8" x 12" sheet of patterned paper into thirds
2. Make half-circle cuts in two flaps and trim with scallop-edged paper, punching holes in top layer of scallop for decorative touch
3. Tie satin ribbon around folded envelope
4. Cut thin sheet of metal to fit inside invitation
5. Using a word processing program, print out wedding details on decorative paper
6. Using decoupage, adhere printed invitation to metal, let dry and seal with decoupage
7. Add flower to bottom of invitation and slip into envelope

Boho chic paper and brad accents (lauren), scallop-edged cardstock paper (in bloom) and metal sheets: Making Memories

Glossy decoupage: Mod Podge by Plaid

Satin eggplant ribbon: Offray

Silk flower: Michaels

PAGE 42 - 43 JOANNA BOLICK

BABY SHOWER INVITATION AND LETTER ACCENT

1. Cut two sheets of paper to the same size, forming card interior and exterior
2. Adhere together, then fold card so that front portion is shorter than bottom portion
3. Decorate exterior with ribbon or trim, safety pin and add jelly
4. Fold patterned paper used for 'grass' in half, then fringe using scissors
5. Attach 'grass' to bottom half of interior by positioning it slightly in front of interior card crease
6. Stamp patterned paper with foam floral stamps, trim to size, add safety pin and tag and adhere to background along with stem
7. Print out invitation information and attach to bottom half of card interior
8. Accent: apply rub-ons to wooden alphabet letter

MM kids paper (kate and ethan) and trims (kate), cardstock paper (springtime), jellies (you're invited), cardstock tags (valentines), scrapbook colors acrylic paint, foam stamps (flower), photo décor decorative letters and safety pins: Making Memories

Computer font: Minion Pro and LainieDaySH

BABY SHOWER CENTERPIECE

1. Stuff shredded 'grass' in transparent container
2. Place floral wire between two stems and adhere together, forming flower stems
3. Create flowers using foam flower stamps, acrylic paint and various patterned papers
4. After paint has dried, trim flowers to size
5. Accessorize flowers with safety pins, cardstock tags, rub-ons and buttons
6. Assemble flowers, then arrange in 'vase'
7. Adhere baby sheer frame and painted chipboard letter 'B' to outside of vase

MM kids paper (kate and ethan), sheer frame (baby), woven ribbon, cardstock tags (valentines), scrapbook colors acrylic paint (sherbet), foam stamps (flower), safety pins, rub-ons wordage (baby) and gameboard alphabet (sadie): Making Memories

PAGE 44 - 45 MAGGIE HOLMES

CONGRATS

1. Create card from orange cardstock
2. Cut green cardstock and blue cardstock to size
3. Cut circles in blue cardstock
4. Layer blue cardstock over green cardstock and stitch with sewing machine
5. Paint chipboard star and attach with dimensional adhesive to card
6. Adhere ribbon charm letters

Cardstock paper, scrapbook colors acrylic paint, chipboard shapes (star), gem stickers and ribbon charm alphabets: Making Memories

Corner rounder and circle cutter: Creative Memories:

Other: thread and sewing machine

NO. 3

1. Cut vellum to size and round corners
2. Paint chipboard letter and apply dimensional glaze
3. Adhere rub-ons and number to vellum
4. Cut photo to same size as vellum and round corners
5. Create announcement in photoshop, matte with orange cardstock and round corners
6. Layer all pieces together and secure with paperclip tied with ribbon

Cardstock paper, rub-ons, chipboard letters, ribbon and scrapbook colors acrylic paint: Making Memories

Corner rounder: Creative Memories

Fonts: Establo and Arial

Diamond glaze: Judi-kins

Other: paperclip

PAGE 46 - 47 LYNNE MONTGOMERY

IT'S A GIRL

1. Adhere two sheets of patterned paper together, patterned side out
2. To make outside folder, fold paper in half and trim down front portion so back shows
3. Round corners
4. Create inserts and trim so verbiage is sticking out a bit from outside folder
5. Secure inserts to folder by creating a hinge in right corner using a brad or eyelet
6. Add ribbons to inserts and embellish folder as desired

Boho chic paper, crystal brads and vintage hip trims (gracen): Making Memories

Other: ribbon and flower

BABY GARLAND

1. Cover left and right side of each cube with decorative paper
2. Create a hole in center of each right and left side big enough to glue a large eyelet grommet
3. String ribbon through holes
4. Cut photos to size (4 needed for each cube) and embellish as desired
5. Adhere photos to cubes

Artistic tags (baby girl), blossoms, boho chic brad accents and paper, gem stickers, photo cubes, rub-ons, safety pins, eyelet grommets and washer words: Making Memories

Other: large eyelets, ribbon and rings

PAGE 48 - 49 KRIS STANGER

BABY JOURNAL

1. Place newborn photo on first page of mini book
2. Blue buttons and add rub-ons to front cover
3. On inside vellum page, add rub-on name and baby sticker embellishments
4. On second page under name, add a metal frame with baby ribbon and baby hand charms
5. Starting with birth month of baby, rub-ons mini; one page per month

Mini book (sky), buttons, rub-ons (love), rub-ons mini (baby and months), rub-ons alphabet (mixed), boho chic frame and baby charms: Making Memories

BABY CARD

1. Trim four different pieces of patterned paper and glue to card
2. Rub white paint over metal charm, then wipe off excess
3. Tie white thread through celery buttons
4. Glue all buttons on horizontal seams of paper
5. Add rub-on under buttons on right side of card

Card, buttons, charmed plaques (baby 2), scrapbook colors acrylic paint (cityscape), stitches (white), rub-ons (baby) and cardstock paper (avenue): Making Memories

PAGE 50 - 51 VICKI BOUTIN

MONOGRAM PHOTO DÉCOR

1. Cut strips of patterned paper and adhere to monogram letter
2. Add ric rac, rub-ons and buttons to monogram letter
3. Paint metal frames with acrylic paint, lightly sand when dry and add photos
4. Cut three varying lengths of ribbon and attach to back side of frames
5. Using decorative scissors, cut three squares of patterned paper slightly larger than frames and adhere to back of each frame

6. Suspend frames from monogram with ribbon brads
7. Add bows to frames

8" chipboard letter, MM kids paper, trims (bella) and buttons, charmed frames, crystal brads, ribbon brads, rub-ons and scrapbook colors acrylic paint: Making Memories

NURSERY MOBILE

1. Paint embroidery hoop and cover with paper
2. Paint metal frames and cover front sides with paper
3. Insert photos and glue ribbon to back of each frame, running up through the embroidery hoop
4. Adhere patterned paper, painted chipboard letters and rub-ons to back of each frame
5. Add chipboard flowers and ribbon to frames
6. Glue bows and metal words to embroidery hoop
7. Gather ribbon at top and stitch a hoop for hanging

Charmed frames, MM kids paper (bella), charmed words, jigsaw alphabet, gameboard shapes (flowers), ribbon, scrapbook colors acrylic paint and rub-ons: Making Memories

Other: embroidery hoop

PAGE 52 - 53 SHERELLE CHRISTENSEN

BABY SHOWER INVITE, DÉCOR AND LAYOUT

1. Layer ribbons and patterned paper in upper corner and stitch into place
2. Cut piece of ledger paper and adhere to lower corner
3. Print journaling and title, cut into strips and adhere
4. Cut mini flower shaped from patterned papers and add ribbon brad for center
5. Add zig zag stitching for flower stems
6. Adhere photo

Ledger paper, MM kids paper, buttons and trims, ribbon brads and simply fabulous trims: Making Memories

Font: Old Type from twopeasinabucket.com and Butterbrotpapier from internet

Ink: Tim Holtz Distressing Ink in antique linen

PAGE 54 KRIS STANGER

BABY HANGERS

1. Sand wooden hangers and paint
2. Once paint is dry, apply coat of mod podge to seal and add shine
3. Embellish with rub-ons, buttons and charms
4. Attach ribbon

Scrapbook colors acrylic paint (springtime and cityscape), rub-ons alphabet (mixed), ribbon, charmed plaques, buttons, rub-ons mini (baby) and vintage hip trims: Making Memories

PAGE 55 JESSICA KOPP AND MARGIE ROMNEY-ASLETT

BABY SHOWER INVITATION

1. Design, print and cut out a 3" x 15" pennant shape
2. Score middle with bone folder
3. Clip pointed end off of shish kebab stick
4. Cover inside of pennant with double sided tape, making sure to put a piece along fold
5. Place stick along fold and close
6. Punch hole in top and tie coordinating ribbon

BABY SHOWER FAVOR BAGS

1. Staple scalloped printed paper to bag and cover with coordinating ribbon

MM kids paper and trims (ethan): Making Memories
Colored paper bag: Michaels
Other: shish kebab sticks (wood/generic)

PAGE 58 - 59 CHRISTY TOMLINSON

NEW YEAR'S PARTY CARD

1. Cut brown cardstock to form square card
2. Matte brown cardstock onto white cardstock
3. Adhere cheeky pebble stickers inside smaller square tags, using tag maker
4. Adhere number stickers to square tan cardstock, sized to fit inside large square tag
5. Complete tag using tag maker
6. Adhere two smaller tags to card first, then adhere larger tag on top
7. Use small rub-ons to create 'Let's Party!'

Cheeky pebble stickers (emery expressions), nothing but numbers (in bloom), tag maker and tag maker rims (square): Making Memories
Cardstock: Bazzill
Rub-ons: Chatterbox

NEW YEAR'S PARTY FAVORS

1. Cut a 4" x 12" strip of cardstock
2. Fold cardstock accordion style in 1" strips
3. Once you make an accordion fan, staple in center
4. Cut a curve across bottom of each side, ending at a point
5. Fan out paper and adhere sides, creating a pinwheel
6. Adhere stick or straw to back of pinwheel and button to center front
7. Create three or four and place them in a glass cup or vase for table display

Cheeky paper (emery): Making Memories
Button: Junkits
Acrylic stick: Target

PAGE 60 - 61 ROBYN WERLICH

SUPER BOWL BASH BETTING GRID

1. Layer papers on 9" x 9" layout, creating a grid
2. Add glitter to letter stickers and ribbon to printed text
3. Cover chipboard stars with paper and add to page

SUPER BOWL BASH PITCHER

1. Add various velvet word stickers and a wide, wire ribbon to pitcher

SUPER BOWL BASH INVITATION

1. Print invitation text on metallic paper, then add wide wire ribbon and strip of paper
2. Using a die cut machine, punch harlequin shapes and add to invitation
3. Add sewing and star brads

Cardstock paper (childhood), MM kids paper (sam) and fresh stickers (sam), all about alphas (spotlight), gameboard shapes (stars), brads (star), velvet sayings stickers (expressions) : Making Memories
Diamond die-cut shape: Quickutz
Thread: Michaels
Fonts: Fragile and Al Uncle from twopeasinabucket.com
Other: metallic paper, sewing, wire, staples and thread

PAGE 62 VICKI BOUTIN

VALENTINE DECORATION

1. Print 'love' and 'be mine' on paper
2. Using tag maker template, cut paper and create heart tag
3. Using decorative scissors, cut two graduating sized hearts from patterned paper
4. Layer tag and heart shapes with dimensional adhesive (glue dots)
5. Add notions and ribbon

Vintage hip paper, buttons, findings and trinket, tag maker and tag maker rims (heart): Making Memories
Other: glue dots

PAGE 63 JIHAE KWON

L O V E

1. Select desired jigsaw shapes
2. Remove cut out shapes and glue tissue paper on back side
3. Glue edges of each shape, forming a lantern
4. Use christmas lights to illuminate (do not use candles)

Cheeky jigsaw patterned alphabet: Making Memories
Other: glue, christmas lights and tissue paper

PAGE 64 - 65 ERIN TERRELL

LOVE BLOSSOMS

1. Cover gameboard hearts with red paper and trim
2. Sand edges
3. Decorate various card backgrounds with patterned paper and ribbon
4. Add gameboard hearts to cards, forming flower shapes
5. Add rub-ons or stickers for finishing touch

Cardstock paper, patterned paper, gameboard shapes (hearts), word fetti, ribbon, jump rings, cardstock tags and rub-ons: Making Memories
Other: chipboard

LOVE NOTES BOX

1. Cover an ordinary shoe box with patterned papers
2. Add gameboard letters and shapes (heart) to spell 'love notes'
3. Add rub-on sentiment to top of box
4. Back sheer frame with red cardstock
5. Trim hole in lid that is the same size as frame opening
6. Glue frame in place

Cardstock paper, boho chic paper (lauren), gameboard shapes (hearts and letters) and rub-ons: Making Memories
Other: heart and striped patterned paper: SEI

PAGE 66 - 67 MELLETTE BEREZOSKI

SWEETHEART CARD

1. Attach blue trim over row of dots on library pocket card, taping ends to back
2. Cut a 5½" x 1" piece of floral paper and adhere above trim, folding and taping ends to back
3. Attach cardstock tags to card with pin
4. Cut a 4⅞" x 4" piece of striped paper
5. Place inside pocket and secure with heart clip

BE MINE CARD

1. Cut a 5" x 1¼" piece of striped paper
2. Adhere striped paper to front of pocket card, folding and taping ends to back
3. Attach trim below striped paper, taping ends to back
4. Attach brads to colorboard label holder and adhere to front of pocket
5. Apply page pebble to blossom, attach to label holder and adhere button to top of tag

Card packs, cheeky paper (emery), page pebble (holiday 1), cardstock tags (love), blossoms (daisy buttercup), vintage hip trims, trinket pins and buttons (gracen) and shaped clip (heart): Making Memories

9 REASONS

1. Cut a square opening from box lid and trim edges with strips of cardstock
2. Adhere a piece of transparency to inside of lid, creating a window
3. Wrap ribbon around lid and tape ends inside
4. Print title on blue cardstock, apply with tag maker and tie to bow
5. Wrap each candy bar with patterned paper, print journaling, attach to front and apply number stickers to each journaling strip

Cheeky paper (emery), MM kids fresh stickers (sam), tag maker and tag maker rims (circle): Making Memories

Box: Red Envelope

Ribbon: Michaels

PAGE 70 - 71 MAGGIE HOLMES

BLOSSOMS CAKE

1. Layer a variety of paper flowers together and insert brads through centers
2. Keep brad prongs closed and insert them right into cake
3. Continue until base of cake circumference is covered

Blossoms, petals and brads: Making Memories

Other: cake stand

SPRING BRANCHES

1. Cut a few branches at different lengths and spray with white paint
2. Poke ends of branches through fabric and flower centers
3. Use scissors to make holes bigger, if necessary
4. Insert branches into glass bottle
5. Adhere ribbon and brad around neck of bottle

Blossoms, petals, brads and ribbon: Making Memories

Other: branches, spray paint and bottle

PAGE 72 - 73 MELLETTE BEREZOSKI

SO MANY EGGS

1. Crop photos and patterned papers to same size square
2. Attach paper and photo blocks, alternating papers, color photos and black and white photos
3. Attach large photo to bottom of collage
4. Print journaling on scallop-edged paper and adhere next to large photo
5. Add embellishments
6. Attach clip to top of collage

Cheeky paper (abby), vintage hip paper, textured cardstock paper (cityscape), enamel tiles, clip, page pebbles, gameboard tags (circle), scrapbook colors acrylic paint (polo club), rub-ons images (love), MM kids buttons (emma), ribbon, ribbon attachment, petals, all about alphas, brad accents and crystal brads: Making Memories

Font: Goudy Old Style, Microsoft Word

Flower punch: EK Success

Orange patterned paper: Scenic Route Paper Co.

DECORATIVE EASTER EGGS

1. Blow out jumbo sized eggs and dye as desired
2. Add mini blossoms and gem stickers to one egg
3. Add rub-ons to a few eggs, adding flower and crystal brads if desired
4. Cut flowers from trim and glue all over egg for a mosaic look
5. Cut small pieces of patterned papers and decoupage to egg for a mosaic look
6. Add letter stickers, ribbons, buttons, petals and buckles

Scrapbook dye, petals, mini blossoms, rub-ons mini, rub-ons images, rub-ons wordage, ribbon, simply fabulous trims, boho chic trims (lauren), MM kids fresh stickers, gem stickers, crystal brads and glue: Making Memories

PAGE 74 - 75 CHRISTY TOMLINSON

GARDEN SEED PACKETS

1. Trace three seed packets onto cardstock and cut out
2. Using decorative scissors, cut along top front and top back for a decorative look
3. Fold and glue into place creating a pocket
4. Print 'rosemary seeds,' 'thyme seeds' and 'sage seeds' onto cardstock and size to fit on small rectangular tag
5. Follow Tag Maker instructions to finish off printed seed tags
6. Adhere one tag to front of each seed packet
7. Attach ribbon or ric rac to front of each packet, then embellish with buttons and pins

MM kids paper (kate and brooke), straight pin (bella) and trims (bella), vintage hip buttons (gracen), blossoms, tag maker, tag metal rims (rectangle) and ribbon: Making Memories

Other: Bazzill cardstock

GARDEN POTS

1. Clean and dry three clay pots
2. Use hammer or file to carefully chip off pieces around top of pots
3. Paint pots with a dry brush technique, leaving parts of clay exposed
4. Sand down edges of pots
5. Use foam stamps to decorate two of the pots
6. Embellish with gems and buttons
7. Apply rub-ons to spell out 'rosemary,' 'thyme' and 'sage' on top of each pot

Vintage hip buttons (gracen), gem stickers (clear), foam stamps (dingbats), scrapbook colors acrylic paint (sherbet, springtime and cityscape): Making Memories

Other: clay pots

PAGE 76 - 77 VICKI BOUTIN

ST. PADDY'S DAY CARD

1. Create card by folding cardstock
2. Ink and layer patterned paper and cream cardstock
3. Create tags and attach to card with brads
4. Draw a thin black border on cream cardstock using a fine-tip black pen
5. Add patterned paper tab with brad to top of tag
6. Place sticker and attach ribbon with staples

Boho chic paper (olivia), tiny alpha stickers, ribbon, tag maker, tag maker rims (heart) and brads: Making Memories

Other: cardstock and brown ink

ST. PADDY'S DAY BROOCH

1. Fold ribbon loops into shamrock shape and staple in place
2. Add strip of ribbon for stem and staple
3. Cut out two circles from patterned paper and use decorative scissors to finish the larger of the two
4. Create a custom metal tag for center with rub-ons and patterned paper
5. Glue pieces together and add pin closure to back

ST. PADDY'S DAY ACCESSORIES

1. Fold ribbon loops into shamrock shape and staple in place
2. Add a strip of ribbon for the stem and staple
3. Create a loop from ribbon and attach to back of shamrock
4. Cut out two circles from patterned paper and use decorative scissors to finish the larger of the two
5. Attach ribbon brad
6. Glue pieces together
7. Feed shoe lace through loop at back and wear

Boho chic paper (olivia), ribbon, ribbon brads, tag maker and tag maker rims (circle): Making Memories

Other: pin closure

PAGE 80 - 81 LYNNE MONTGOMERY

GRANDMA'S BRAG BOX

1. Decoupage lunch tin with patterned paper using decoupage and collage gel
2. Adhere scalloped sticker border and gingham ribbon around upper rim of tin
3. Thread narrow ribbons through latch hole and tie in bow
4. Attach walnut-inked tag and heart charm to bow with jump ring
5. Create inserts by walnut-inking manila 'a' through 'z' tabs, which can be purchased at an office supply store
6. Embellish cards with names and photos of each child and/or grandchild
7. When photos are received, simply tuck them behind corresponding index cards in box

Dyeable shipping tag, jump ring, ribbon, safety pins, rub-ons, vintage hip border stickers, buttons and paper: Making Memories

Decoupage and collage gel: Crafter's Pick

Oxford A-Z card guides: Esselte

Walnut ink: Post Modern Design

Other: chenille material, heart charm and label maker name stickers

HAPPY MOTHER'S DAY

1. Fold walnut-inked paper matchbook style
2. Apply rub-on greeting to a walnut-inked shipping tag
3. Sew strips of patterned paper to front of matchbook card, catching bottom of shipping tag in middle strip
4. Use a ruler to make straight edge tears on all sewn strips
5. Add an eyelet to top portion of matchbook, securing top flap (make sure to line up placement of eyelet with hole in shipping tag but don't connect the two)
6. Close card by threading ribbon through eyelet and shipping tag
7. Embellish with flowers and brads

Blossoms, dyeable shipping tag, brads (heart), ribbon, rub-ons and vintage hip paper: Making Memories

Walnut ink: Post Modern Design

Other: ¼" eyelet

PAGE 82 GAIL PIERCE-WATNE

MY FAMILY

1. Cover back of shadowbox with choice of paper
2. Attach binder rings to base on top of back paper
3. Punch holes on pages to fit rings

Boho chic paper and trims: Making Memories

Other: shadowbox by Pottery Barn

PAGE 83 SHERELLE CHRISTENSEN

MOTHER'S DAY ALBUM

1. Cut patterned paper to fit front of album and adhere
2. Embellish cover using stickers and trims
3. Adhere stickers and patterned paper to inside pages of album
4. Add photos and embellishments

Boho chic paper, stickers, trims, mini album and decorative brads: Making Memories

Tags: Avery

Ink: Tim Holtz distress ink in antique linen

Other: vintage button

PAGE 84 - 85 MELLETTE BEREZOSKI

FATHER'S DAY CARDS

1. For grandfather card, attach espresso paper and ribbon to front of manila matchbook style card
2. Print journaling on white cardstock and attach, slightly overlapping ribbon and espresso paper
3. Add photo anchor, colorboard sticker frame, watch hands, charmed phrase and leather lacing
4. For dad card: cut a 4½" x 5½" piece of brown tweed paper
5. Cut a 4½" x 4½" piece of sky cardstock and layer with father sticker, dot, stripe and plaid paper
6. Sew sky cardstock piece over brown tweed piece
7. Add ribbon, chipboard letter and metal phrase charm

Boho chic paper (lauren), MM kids paper (ethan), colorboard frame, like it is stickers, charmed phrases, photo anchor, ribbon, brads and chipboard alphabet: Making Memories

Clock hands: Walnut Hollow

EDWARD LEE BEREZOSKI

1. Adhere patterned papers, ribbon and journaling strip to front of clipboard
2. Cut large photo into a circle, attach to clipboard and trim off excess at corner
3. Use tag maker to convert small photos into round, metal-rimmed tags
4. Use circle cutter to cut two circles from patterned papers and add rub-on wordage
5. Arrange photos and paper circles on clipboard as desired and attach
6. Add additional circular embellishments, some overlapping the photos or paper circles

MM kids paper (ethan), boho chic paper (lauren), cardstock paper (avenue cool grey), tag maker, tag maker rims, ribbon, vintage hip buttons, charmed enamel, washer words, brads, rub-ons wordage and gameboard shapes (heart): Making Memories

Clipboard: 7 Gypsies

Globe accent: Magic Scraps

PAGE 86 - 87 JIHAE KWON

CHANG FAMILY REUNION INVITATION

1. Layout type on computer and print
2. Mount on coordinating background
3. Punch a hole near top
4. Thread ribbon through hole, attach with brad and secure using tape on back of invitation

MM kids paper, ribbon and ribbon brads (max) and textured cardstock paper (cityscape and sherbet): Making Memories

CHANG FAMILY REUNION COASTERS

1. Create a design with last name on computer and print
2. Cut a piece of cardstock and mount printout on top
3. Cut a piece of ribbon and insert brad
4. Slide cardstock piece into photo décor coaster
5. Tape ribbon piece on back of coaster

MM kids paper, ribbon and ribbon brads (max), textured cardstock paper (sherbet) and photo décor coasters: Making Memories

CHANG FAMILY REUNION KEEPSAKE BOX

1. Cover box with cardstock
2. Cut ¾" wide strips of paper
3. Glue strips to lid in woven pattern
4. Print last name and cut to fit inside tag maker rim
5. Create tag
6. Cut a small piece of ribbon and insert brad
7. Place ribbon piece on bottom corner of lid and place tag on top

MM kids paper, ribbon and ribbon brads (max), textured cardstock paper (sherbet), tag maker rims and tag maker: Making Memories

Other: box

PAGE 90 - 91 MAGGIE HOLMES

4TH OF JULY

1. Create invitation in photoshop and matte with blue cardstock
2. Cut a strip of vellum long enough to wrap around invitation and secure with staples
3. Coat chipboard stars first with silver paint, then again with glitter paint
4. Adhere stars to vellum, then slide vellum band around invitation

Cardstock paper, chipboard shapes and vellum: Making Memories

Paint: Delta and DecoArt

Font: Tahoma, Fabianestem and Verdana

4TH OF JULY PINWHEEL

1. Adhere two sheets of paper back to back, making sure it is secure
2. Cover chipboard star with silver paint, then again with glitter paint
3. Cut paper into a square
4. Fold square corner to corner, then unfold
5. Make a pencil mark about ⅓ of the way from center
6. Cut along fold lines stopping at pencil mark
7. Bring every other point into center and stick brad through star and all four points to secure

Cardstock paper, patterned paper, chipboard star and crystal brads: Making Memories

Paint: Delta and DecoArt

PAGE 92 - 93 MELLETTE BEREZOSKI

FLIP FLOP CENTERPIECE

1. Decorate each flip flop as desired (try petals, ribbon, colorboard stickers, charmed enamel and rub-ons)
2. Cut a 24" piece of chipboard at ½" wide
3. Hot glue strip of chipboard to back of one flip flop (towards toe end), fold chipboard where next flip flop starts and glue to second flip flop
4. Continue gluing chipboard strip to all six flip flops, forming a hexagon and overlapping ends
5. Reinforce chipboard strip to flip flops by pushing flat head thumbtacks through chipboard strip
6. Use polo club paints to stamp flowers onto textured cardstock
7. Trim around flowers, embellish centers and glue to bamboo skewers

Textured cardstock paper (polo club), scrapbook colors acrylic paint (polo club), petals, rub-ons images (beach), ribbon, metal signage, colorboard stickers (summer), enamel tiles (summer), foam stamps, crystal brads and ribbon brads: Making Memories

Flip flops: Michaels

Other: chipboard, thumbtacks and bamboo skewers

POOL PARTY INVITATION

1. Cut a 10" square piece of lagoon cardstock
2. From all four edges, mark 2½" towards center, which leave a 5" square in center of page
3. Trim four flaps outside the 5" square into half circles
4. Score and fold at the 5" square markings
5. Adhere lemon and apricot dot paper to two of the flaps and lagoon and kiwi flower paper to remaining two flaps, trimming excess paper
6. Computer print invitation on white cardstock and attach to inside of card
7. Wrap card with vellum band and add ribbon, circle tag and enamel charm

Textured cardstock paper (polo club), cardstock paper (polo club), MM kids trims (emma), charmed enamel (girlie girl), metal rim tag (circle brights), colorboard stickers (summer), vellum, mini blossoms and crystal brads: Making Memories

Font: Franklin Gothic Book and Bitstream Vera Serif, Microsoft Word

Digital brushes: NSD Cheer and Old Stamps by Rhonna Farrer from twopeasinabucket.com

PAGE 94 - 95 KRIS STANGER

SUMMER PARTY DÉCOR COLLAGE

1. Take two 9" x 9" pieces of cardstock and cut one exactly in half
2. Score both ends of cut pieces at jagged edge
3. Attach one piece at top with brads and the other at bottom with blue
4. Add wallet-size photos of coaches on front along with team photo
5. Open to inside, adding wallet photos of each teammate and journaling their names and player numbers
6. Add rub-ons to circle tags along with ribbon and attach

Cardstock paper (harvest), rub-ons (sports), MM kids buttons, ribbon (green), rub-ons images (love), rub-ons alphabet (mixed), rub-ons mini (sport) and tagged circles (black and white): Making Memories

SUMMER PARTY DÉCOR SPORTS BANNER

1. Cut six 12" x 12" sheets of linen cardstock in half
2. Find center of 6" x 12" paper and cut at an angle, creating flag (save scraps for place setting flags)
3. Fold ½" flap over at tops of flags, trim edge and glue down over ribbon
4. Stamp wording onto flags
5. Add mini brads to top of flags
6. Add ribbon by knotting between flags

Scrapbook colors acrylic paint (cityscape), textured cardstock paper (childhood), foam stamps (simply fabulous), mini brads and ribbon: Making Memories

PAGE 96 - 97 JULIE TURNER

PARTY LIGHTS

1. Create your own template for paper shades, then trace, cut and score
2. Center opening size may need to be adjusted depending on size of party lights used
3. Fold pleated shades and use decorative scissors to cut an edge on plain shades
4. Punch small holes in shades so light can shine through
5. Securely wrap shade around light and glue along edge
6. Add small amount of glue around top of shade to secure to light and keep aligned
7. Embellish with ribbon tie

MM kids paper and trims: Making Memories

String of party lights: Target

GARDEN PARTY INVITATION

1. Print invitations on cardstock, leaving enough space on left margin for accordion pleat
2. Pleat left margin and decorate with thin strips of patterned paper
3. Glue a charmed enamel flower onto pleat
4. Stamp flower in bottom right corner
5. Punch out small flower from patterned paper and glue to center of stamped flower

MM kids paper, charmed enamel (flowers) and foam stamps (flower): Making Memories

Ink: Stampin' Up

GARDEN PARTY NAPKIN

1. Use foam stamps and a heat-setting pigment ink to stamp designs onto paper napkins

Foam stamps (flower): Making Memories

Paper napkins: IKEA

Ink: Stampin' Up

GARDEN PARTY NAPKIN CUPCAKE TOPPER

1. Punch a circle from patterned paper
2. Glue a charmed enamel onto flower
3. Glue a painted toothpick to back of circle and stick into cupcake

MM kids paper, charmed enamel (flowers) and scrapbook colors acrylic paint: Making Memories

PAGE 100 - 101 MAGGIE HOLMES

BOO

1. Create party invitation in photoshop and print on transparency
2. Cut orange cardstock to size
3. Cut white cardstock to size and fold in half, layering around transparency and orange cardstock
4. Attach strip of patterned paper and velvet letter stickers
5. Punch holes, then thread bead chain and tag through holes
6. Tie ribbon onto bead chain

Cardstock paper, patterned paper, colorboard stickers, bead chain and velvet alphabet stickers: Making Memories

Ribbon: American Crafts

Font: InaiMathi and Cracked

HALLOWEEN PLACEMAT AND NAPKIN RING

1. Cut strip of orange cardstock and punch circles
2. Layer black patterned paper behind and stitch with sewing machine
3. Attach strip to left side of patterned paper and adorn with alphabet fetti and colorboard sticker
4. For napkin ring, repeat steps one and two, then cut strip to desired length
5. Matte strip with alternating color and staple together
6. Adorn napkin ring with word fetti stickers

Cardstock paper, colorboard stickers, patterned paper, word fetti and alphabet fetti: Making Memories

Corner rounder: Creative Memories

Other: thread, sewing machine and circle punch

PAGE 102 - 103 ERIN TERRELL

BOO SCRAPBOOK LAYOUT

1. Trim 9" x 9" background out of cardstock
2. Add various photos to showcase halloween through the years
3. Trim patterned paper and ribbons for borders
4. Add rub-ons, stickers and metal accents
5. Place small envelopes on page
6. Cover chipboard letters with black paint and allow to dry
7. Add chipboard letters and brads to envelopes

Brads, cardstock paper, charmed enamel, colorboard stickers, patterned paper, word fetti (halloween), scrapbook colors acrylic paint and rub-ons mini: Making Memories

Ribbon: Michaels

Envelopes: Bazzill Basics cardstock

BOO CANDY BAG

1. Download a bag template from any site on internet
2. Trace onto back side of halloween patterned paper
3. Cut out bag and assemble
4. Trim top of bag with pinking shears

Patterned paper (halloween): Making Memories

Scissors: Provo Craft

BOO INVITATION AND CANDY DISHES

1. Spray paint buckets with black chalkboard paint and allow to dry
2. Once dry, use double sided tape to adhere ribbon trim along top border
3. Trim card out of orange cardstock
4. Place patterned paper and ribbon along bottom border and inside of card
5. Place patterned paper and ribbon along bottom border of envelope
6. Add 'cat' rub-on to card
7. Add 'boo' charmed enamel to window of card

Charmed enamel (halloween), rub-ons mini (cat) and patterned paper (halloween): Making Memories

Card envelope: Bazzill Basics

Patterned paper: Chatterbox

Ribbon: Michaels

PAGE 104 - 105 CHRISTY TOMLINSON

HALLOWEEN PLACE SETTING

1. Adhere 'happy halloween' rub-on around outside edge of plate charger and place gems in between any repeated sayings
2. Tie ribbons and the letter 'h' around base of goblet, placing gem on alphabet
3. Gather and tie silverware together with ribbon
4. Cut a small piece of cardstock, add letter 'h' sticker on top and punch hole in corner for threading of ribbon
5. For place card, cut and fold cardstock in half, adding an accent strip of patterned paper across top half
6. Use rub-on and pen for guest's initials
7. Place two gems under left hand side of patterned paper strip

Rub-ons alphabet (misunderstood and circus), ribbon (black, orange and halloween), monograms (metal), gem stickers (clear) and velvet alphabet stickers (black): Making Memories

Cardstock: Bazzill

Other: charger, goblet and silverware

HALLOWEEN CANDY VASE

1. Clean glass vase
2. List halloween words for use on vase
3. Start on one side and work your way around, placing a mixture of rub-on sizes, styles and colors
4. Overlap some words to create a continuous effect
5. Fill jar half-way with candy corn or other treats
6. Set candle on top of candy

Rub-ons alphabet: Making Memories

Other: glass hurricane lamp

PAGE 106 - 107 ERIN TERRELL

GIVE THANKS TRAY

1. Take photos of thanksgiving decorations and size them
2. Print photos with extra white border to fit inside tray
3. Add textured paper and ribbon along bottom border
4. Add rub-ons below photos and on ribbon
5. Place stickers in upper left corner and on ribbon border

Colorboard stickers, ribbon and rub-ons: Making Memories

Ribbon (striped): Michaels

Rub-ons (joyful and memories) and stickers (round epoxy stickers): SEI

Other: textured paper

FAMILY MEMORIES

1. Remove clock apparatus, then cover matte board with textured paper
2. Add decorative ribbon through photo opening
3. Add decorative labels, flowers and rub-ons
4. Insert photo
5. Spray paint clock dial black and allow to dry
6. Trim decorative paper and matte to create background
7. Add numbers to clock, then reassemble clock dial and background

Cardstock paper, photo décor photo clock, mini blossoms and rub-ons: Making Memories

Family Memories: MAMBI

Ribbon: Michaels

Spray paint: Krylon

Other: textured paper

PAGE 110 - 111 *ERIN TERRELL*

JOY CARD SET

1. Trim two cards to 6" x 8", then score along the 4" mark (to create 4" x 6" card front)
2. Add patterned papers to card fronts, as shown
3. Add ribbon and sticker accents to card fronts
4. On one of the cards, add patterned paper to chipboard letters, then trim
5. Sand edges of chipboard letters, then place on card front

Jigsaw alphabet (poolside), colorboard stickers (winter), patterned paper (winter), ribbon, and sandpaper: Making Memories

Patterned paper: Scenic Route (on the interior of one of the cards)

TREE CARD SET

1. Trim 2 cards to 8½" x 7", then score along the 4¼" mark (to create 4¼" x 7" card front)
2. Add patterned papers to card fronts, as shown
3. Use circle punch to create circles for tree shape
4. Add one circle of a contrasting color
5. Add stickers or patterned paper for tree base
6. Add ribbon along bottom strip of patterned paper

Stickers (christmas) patterned paper (winter) and ribbon: Making Memories

Circle punch: Family Treasures

PAGE 112 - 113 *MAGGIE HOLMES*

HAPPY HOLIDAYS

1. Cut two squares from patterned paper and remove inside portion, leaving a frame
2. Cut piece of transparency to sandwich between two frames and adhere together
3. Stitch square with sewing machine
4. Create card in photoshop and print
5. Create polka dot effect with either foam stamps and paint or an embossing template
6. Adhere enamel charm to polka dot square, round corners and adhere to center of transparency
7. Adhere message square to back side of card, making sure everything is aligned

Cardstock paper, patterned paper (holiday and winter), foam stamp and charmed enamel: Making Memories

Corner rounder: Creative Memories

Paint: Delta

Rubber stamp: Paper Salon

Font: Establo

Other: thread, sewing machine and transparencies

HOLIDAY CARDS

1. Create greeting in photoshop and print on white cardstock
2. Round corners and matte with patterned paper
3. Print photo to fit on card and adhere and stitch with sewing machine
4. Print shape onto piece of paper, cut out and trace onto chipboard
5. Cut out chipboard shape and cover with a combination of either patterned paper and diamond glaze or microbeads and diamond glaze

Cardstock paper and patterned paper (winter): Making Memories

Corner rounder: Creative Memories

Microbeads: Provo Craft

Diamond glaze: Judi-kins

Font: Impact

Other: thread and sewing machine

PAGE 114 - 115 *MELLETTE BEREZOSKI*

SHEER CHRISTMAS CARDS

1. Cut a sheet of thin plexiglas (available at most arts and crafts stores) with a craft knife and ruler, measuring the standard card size of 4½" x 5½"
2. Tie ribbon to left edge of sheer frame
3. Cut a 1⅝" x 1⅝" piece of patterned paper and adhere to back of frame to cover opening
4. Cut a 3½" x 3½" piece of coordinating patterned paper, round off corners and adhere to plexiglas
5. Attach sheer frame centered on patterned paper square
6. Attach charmed enamel shape and gem sticker inside sheer frame window
7. Apply rub-ons directly to plexiglas below sheer frame

Patterned paper (holiday), sheer frames, charmed enamel (christmas), rub-ons wordage (winter holidays), rub-ons mini (christmas 3), ribbon (vintage hip) and gem stickers: Making Memories

Plexiglas: Hobby Lobby, Crafts Etc.

FROM OUR HOME TO YOURS

1. Using a computer photo program, format text on 2" x 2" photo and print
2. Adhere photo to a 2⅝" x 2⅝" piece of patterned paper and round off corners
3. Attach noel enamel charm to center of photo
4. Attach eyelet to top of photo and string quilting thread through

5. Carefully roll piece, starting from bottom, then slide into clear glass ornament
6. With tweezers, gently unroll and flatten piece
7. String thread through ornament lid, tie in knot and trim off ends

Patterned paper (winter), charmed enamel, ribbon and eyelet: Making Memories

Clear glass ornaments: D&F Designs

PAGE 116 - 117 *JENNIFER JENSEN*

PEACE, LOVE AND JOY

1. Lightly trace inside frame square onto cardstock
2. Spell peace, joy and love with rub-on letters
3. Trim photo or cardstock words to a 2½" square to fit back of frame and adhere (if using photo, back with cardstock)
4. Paint star, tree, holly and snowflake, then align and adhere to front and back center of frame with metal glue
5. Place jump ring through both metal eyelet charms and secure
6. Tie ribbon onto jump ring

Rub-ons alphabet (mixed), cardstock paper, charmed metal frames, eyelet charms, gem stickers, jump rings, metal glue, scrapbook colors acrylic paint and ribbon: Making Memories

CHLOE AND MIA

1. Cut a 4" x 8½" rectangle from a 12" x 12" page and adhere pink baroque paper underneath
2. Place tag between second and third photos
3. Adhere an 8" piece of boho chic crinkled ribbon with liquid adhesive and place on left side of holiday tag
4. Gently pinch ribbon together with fingers, gathering and creating ruffle
5. Adhere top piece of velvet ribbon to ruffled ribbon and place on right side of holiday tag
6. Add lettering and stamped date

Rub-ons alphabet (mixed), artistic tags, boho chic alphabet stickers, trims and paper (olivia), crystal brads, magnetic stamps and simply fabulous trims: Making Memories

Name strips: Dymo

PAGE 118 - 119 JOANNA BOLICK

HOLIDAY CENTERPIECE

1. Remove photo wreath from box and place face up on table
2. Tie small strands of various ribbons around branches
3. Attach buttons, crystal brads and gems amongst berries
4. Attach safety pins to knotted ribbons
5. Embellish three candles and place in center of wreath

Photo décor wreath kit, crystal brads (clear circle and square red wagon), woven ribbon (red and white), blossoms (poinsettias), vintage hip buttons, findings and alphabet stickers (gracen), MM kids trims (sam), ribbon card, safety pins, simply fabulous gem stickers (brooke) and buckles and naked line trims: Making Memories

CHRISTMAS STOCKINGS

1. Draw or print out stocking template that fits on an 8½" x 11" sheet of white paper
2. Cut out stocking template to use as pattern and trace two pieces of felt slightly larger than pattern
3. Decorate template with overlapping strips of patterned paper
4. Sew patterned papers at seams using zigzag stitches
5. Straight-stitch or hand-sew two pieces of felt to patterned paper, leaving top of stocking open
6. Trim excess felt from edges
7. Adorn stocking with ribbon hanger and other accents

Patterned paper (holiday and winter), stickers (holiday), vintage hip trims and woven ribbon (red and white): Making Memories

Other: white felt

PAGE 120 JENNY WESTON

NEIGHBOR GIFTS CARD

1. Trim a 5½" x 8½" piece of meadow cardstock and fold to create card
2. Trim a ½" x 5½" piece of lauren tweed paper
3. Trim a 1" x 5½" piece of holly paper and trim one end with decorative scissors
4. Mount paper, ribbon and colorboard on card as shown

Mini colorboard stickers (holiday), boho chic paper (lauren), patterned paper (holiday), cardstock paper (in bloom) and trims (winter): Making Memories

Other: maxicuts wave

NEIGHBOR GIFTS CHOCOLATE DIPPED PRETZEL

1. Melt caramels in a double boiler pan on stove (cook on low to medium heat once it starts to melt so it doesn't become too hard), then stir in 1 tsp. of water
2. Dip each pretzel rod about ⅔ of the way in caramel, spread smooth with a spatula or the back of a spoon and place on parchment paper until set
3. Melt milk chocolate in double broiler pan on stove (cook on low to medium heat so it does not burn)
4. Melt white chocolate in a double broiler pan on stove at the same time
5. Once caramel has set, dip each pretzel rod in milk chocolate
6. Decorate pretzels
   a. Place your sprinkles or candies on a paper plate and roll each pretzel rod in desired topping (or just sprinkle on)
   b. Dip a fork into white chocolate and drizzle over milk chocolate by gently swishing fork back and forth over rods but not touching them
   c. Lay back on parchment paper to set completely

PAGE 121 GAIL PIERCE-WATNE

25 DAYS OF CHRISTMAS

1. Create or find a shallow container or small shadowbox and divide into 24 sections
2. Choose a few coordinating papers to embellish drawer fronts or back of sectioned compartments
3. Number each section from 1 to 24
4. Embellish with trim
5. Put a surprise in each section to be opened each day leading up to christmas.
6. Tie outside of container with a beautiful ribbon

Vintage hip trims and paper, rub-ons, rub-ons images and foam stamps: Making Memories

Wide ribbon: Michaels

PAGE 122 - 123 CHRISTY TOMLINSON

CHRISTMAS CARD HOLDER

1. Paint canvas
2. Cut four strips of 12" paper with various heights
3. Use sewing machine or embroidery thread to stitch design around sides of each strip
4. Starting at top and working your way down, adhere strips of cardstock onto canvas, only applying glue to sides and bottom of each strip
5. Cut and glue strips of ribbon to tops of each paper strip for a finished look
6. Glue buttons at random intervals down each side of ribbon
7. Tie ribbon around corsage pins and insert into ribbons and trims

Patterned paper (holiday) and ribbon (holiday), vintage hip buttons and trinkets and scrapbook colors acrylic paint (spring time): Making Memories

Canvas: Canvas Concepts

Other: sewing machine

CHRISTMAS BLOCKS

1. Cut four blocks for each letter in the word 'noel' and dry brush with paint on the sides, back and outer edge of front
2. Cut patterned paper slightly smaller than main side of blocks and adhere to front
3. Cut and paint smaller chipboard pieces where letters will eventually be stamped
4. Use mixture of foam stamp styles for each letter in the word 'noel'
5. Adorn appropriate chipboard letter with ribbon or buttons before adhering to block
6. Embellish remaining blocks with ribbon and buttons
7. Spray with clear coat, protecting paint and project

Patterned paper (holiday), boho chic trims, cheeky trims (abby), vintage hip buttons and trinkets, simply fabulous gem stickers (clear) and scrapbook colors acrylic paint (childhood, cityscape and springtime): Making Memories

Other: chipboard, clear coat sealer spray and paint brushes

MELLETTE BEREZOSKI
CROSBY, TEXAS

Mellette is a stay-at-home mom and reality-TV junkie who admits that she's a messy scrapbooker but likes to clean up in between projects. When not working on an assignment, you'll most likely find her on her back porch browsing through mail order catalogs, flipping through her old book collection or admiring her flower garden.

LYNNE MONTGOMERY
GILBERT, ARIZONA

Lynne's most recent accomplishment is that she ran in her first 10 mile race. And she had plenty of time to train since she hasn't watched television in the last five years. She is an avid collector of hair magazines, loves homemade blackberry pie and can hardly buy anything without a coupon.

MAGGIE HOLMES
SOUTH JORDAN, UTAH

Even though she's the mother of three boys, Maggie is all girl. A self-confessed fashionista, she's currently working on expanding her growing collection of purses and bags. Always cheerful, smiling and organized, the one thing she'd have if she were stranded on a desert island would be TiVO.

KRIS STANGER
ST. GEORGE, UTAH

To Kris, there's nothing finer than a good pedicure and manicure. Since she's the mother of four, including a newborn, a little pampering is just what she deserves. Other loves include Bath and Body Concentrated Room Spray, planting flowers in the spring, Oprah and the color green in every shade.

JENNIFER JENSEN
HURRICANE, UTAH

A self-described Coke-only drinker (no diet!), Jennifer is terrified of snakes, mice and heights. But that doesn't stop her from doing the things she loves – trailer camping, cooking and baking, eating eggs for breakfast, exercising and talking on the phone for hours.

ERIN TERRELL
SAN ANTONIO, TEXAS

Originally from South Carolina, Erin confesses that her least favorite household chore is cleaning up her scrapbook room. She'd much rather be enjoying the spring weather, reading InStyle magazine, grilling outside, traveling or taking landscape photography.